The
ISO 9001:2000
Auditor's Companion

Also Available from ASQ Quality Press

The ISO 9001:2000 Audit Kit
Kent A. Keeney

The Quality Audit Handbook, Second Edition
J.P. Russell, editing director

The TL 9000 Guide for Auditors
Mark Kempf

ISO 9000:2000 for Small and Medium Businesses
Herbert C. Monnich

Interpreting ISO 9001:2000 with Statistical Methodology
By James L. Lamprecht

ISO 9001:2000 Explained, Second Edition
Joesph J. Tsiakals, Charles A. Cianfrani, and John E. (Jack) West

ISO 9000:2000 Quick Reference
Jeanne Ketola and Kathy Roberts

ISO Lesson Guide 2000: Pocket Guide to Q9001:2000, Second Edition
Dennis Arter and J.P. Russell

ANSI/ISO/ASQ Q9000:2000 Series Quality Standards

The
ISO 9001:2000
Auditor's Companion

Kent A. Keeney

ASQ Quality Press
Milwaukee, Wisconsin

Library of Congress Cataloging-in-Publication Data

Keeney, Kent A., 1947-
  ISO 9001:2000 : auditor's companion / Kent A. Keeney.
    p. cm.
Includes bibliographical references.
  ISBN 0-87389-494-4 (soft cover)
  1. ISO 9000 Series Standards. 2. Quality assurance--Standards--United
States. 3. Quality control--Standards--United States. 4.
Manufactures--Qualtiy control--Standards--United States. I. Title.
  TS156.6 .K45 2001
  658.5'62'021873--dc21

                                                        2001004748

Acquisitions Editor: Annemieke Koudstaal
Project Editor: Craig S. Powell
Production Coordinator: Gretchen Trautman
Special Marketing Representative: Denise Cawley

ASQ Mission: The American Society for Quality advances individual, organizational and community
excellence worldwide through learning, quality improvement and knowledge exchange.

Attention: Bookstores, Wholesalers, Schools and Corporations:
ASQ Quality Press books, videotapes, audiotapes, and software are available at quantity discounts
with bulk purchases for business, educational, or instructional use. For information, please contact
ASQ Quality Press at 800-248-1946, or write to ASQ Quality Press, P.O. Box 3005, Milwaukee, WI
53201-3005.

To place orders or to request a free copy of the ASQ Quality Press Publications Catalog, including
ASQ membership information, call 800-248-1946. Visit our Web site at http://www.asq.org or
http://qualitypress.asq.org.

Printed in the United States of America

 Printed on acid-free paper

American Society for Quality

Quality Press
600 N. Plankinton Avenue
Milwaukee, Wisconsin 53203
Call toll free 800-248-1946
Fax 414-272-1734
www.asq.org
http://qualitypress.asq.org
http://standardsgroup.asq.org
E-mail: authors@asq.org

Foreword

This year marks the second set of revisions to the ISO 9000 Series Standards. These revisions are more extensive and will have far more impact than the revisions to the 1987 version. The year 2000 revisions not only altered the clause numbering, they include changes that require auditors to be more skillful and perceptive. The eight quality management principles will aid in understanding the intent behind most of the year 2000 revisions. The eight quality management principles are:

1. Customer–focused organization

2. Leadership

3. Involvement of people

4. Process approach

5. System approach to management

6. Continual improvement

7. Factual approach to decision making

8. Mutually beneficial supplier relationships

This book, *The ISO 9001:2000 Auditor's Companion* will greatly assist auditors in adjusting to auditing to the new requirements. The practical approach that Kent uses in the "Author's Notes" provides a common sense explanation not often found in other books on this topic. The redline strikeout text comparison is invaluable to anyone wishing to gain a first hand, in-depth understanding of each change.

This book is a key reference for all quality professionals. It is a great tool for assessment, training, and implementation of the new requirements.

Liz Potts
Vice President, Business Development
Ashland Specialty Chemical Co,
Columbus, OH

Acknowledgments

Several people provided help, inspiration, and encouragement to accomplish this work. First and foremost my wife, Paula, spent countless hours over the computer entering, editing, and proofreading the manuscript. I particularly acknowledge the patience and understanding of our son Kurt.

Thanks to Mark Ristow for his help in developing the redline/strikeout comparison, line numbers, and word references.

Thanks also to Kay Smith, Kylie Buzzard, Diane Montanile-Madden, and Greg Spencer for their support and the audits we have performed together.

Additionally, I wish to acknowledge and thank Liz Potts for the foreword.

Thanks to Julie McCaughey, Mike Cox, and Mike Touhey for their comments of appreciation for this book and permission to use them.

AMERICAN NATIONAL STANDARD

Quality management systems—
Model for Quality Assurance in Design, Development, Production, Installation, and Servicing

Requirements

[Revision of first edition (ANSI/ASQC Q91–1987)]
Prepared by
American Society for Quality Control Standards Committee
for
American National Standards Committee Z–1 on Quality Assurance

Approved as a American National Standard by:
American Society for Quality

An American National Standard Approved on August 1, 1994 December 13, 2000

Descriptors: quality assurance , quality assurance program, quality systems, design, development (work), production, installation, after-sales services, reference models.

American National Standards: An American National Standard implies a consensus of those substantially concerned with its scope and provisions. An American National Standard is intended as a guide to aid the manufacturer, the consumer, and the general public. The existence of an American National Standard does not in any respect preclude anyone, whether he or she has approved the standard or not, from manufacturing, purchasing, or using products, processes, or procedures not conforming to the standard. American National Standards are subject to periodic review and users are cautioned to obtain the latest edition.

Caution Notice: This American National Standard may be revised or withdrawn at any time. The procedures of the American National Standards Institute require that action be taken to reaffirm, revise, or withdraw this standard no later than five years from the date of publication. Purchasers of American National Standards may receive current information on all standards by calling or writing the American National Standards Institute.

Table of Contents—1994 and 2000 Versions Merged

Page

Foreword v

Acknowledgments vii

Table of Contents—1994 and 2000 versions merged xi

Table of Contents—2000 version xv

Foreword xix

Preface xxi

Conventions xxiii
    Text conventions xxiii
    Typeface xxiii
    Meaning xxiii
    Footnotes xxiii
    Language xxiii
    Line numbers xxiii
    Order xxiii
    Punctuation xxiii

Introduction 1
    0.1 .... General 1
    0.2 .... Process approach 1
    0.3 .... Relationship with ISO 9004 3
    0.4 .... Compatibility with other management systems 3

1 .... Scope 5
    1.1 .... General 5
    1.2 .... Application 5

2 .... Normative reference 6

3 .... Terms and definitions 6
    3.1 .... product: 6
    3.2 .... tender: 6
    3.3 .... contract; accepted order: 6

4 .... Quality management system requirements 7
    4.1 .... General requirements 7
    4.2 .... Quality system Documentation requirements 10
        4.2.1 .... General 10
        4.2.2 .... Quality-system procedures 10
        4.2.2 .... Quality manual 13
        4.2.3 4.5 .... Document and data Control of documents 14
        4.5.1 .... General 14
        4.5.2 .... Document and data approval and issue 14
        4.5.3 .... Document and data changes 14
        4.2.4 4.16 .... Control of quality records 16

Table of Contents—1994 and 2000 Versions Merged

5 4.1 .... Management responsibility..17
5.1 .... Management commitment 17
5.2 .... Customer focus 18
5.3 4.1.1 .... Quality policy 18
5.4 .... Planning 20
   5.4.1 .... Quality objectives 20
   5.4.2 .... Quality management system planning 20
5.5 4.1.2 .... Organization Responsibility, authority and communication 21
   5.5.1 4.1.2.1 ...... Responsibility and authority 21
   5.5.2 4.1.2.3 ...... Management representative 22
   5.5.3 .... Internal communication 23
5.6 4.1.3 .... Management review 24
   5.6.1 .... General 24
   5.6.2 .... Review input 25
   5.6.3 .... Review output 26

6 .... Resource management 26
6.1 4.1.2.2 .... Provision of resources 26
6.2 .... Human resources 27
   6.2.1 .... General 27
   6.2.2 4.18 .... Competence, awareness and training 28
6.3 .... Infrastructure 29
6.4 .... Work environment 29

7 .... Product realization 30
7.1 .... Planning of product realization 30
7.2 .... Customer-related processes 33
4.3 .... Contract review 33
   4.3.1 .... General 33
   7.2.1 .... Determination of requirements related to the product 33
   7.2.2 4.3.2 .... Review of requirements related to the product 34
   4.3.4 .... Records 34
   4.3.3 .... Amendment to contract 34
   7.2.3 .... Customer communication 36
7.3 4.4 .... Design control and development 36
   4.4.1 .... General 36
   7.3.1 4.4.2 .... Design and development planning 36
   4.4.3 .... Organizational and technical interfaces 36
   7.3.2 4.4.4 .... Design and development inputs 38
   7.3.3 4.4.5 .... Design and development outputs 39
   7.3.4 4.4.6 .... Design and development review 40
   7.3.5 4.4.7 .... Design and development verification 41
   7.3.6 4.4.8 .... Design and development validation 42
   7.3.7 4.4.9 .... Control of design and development changes.............43

7.4 4.6 .... Purchasing 44

    7.4.1 4.6.1 .... General Purchasing process 44

    4.6.2 .... Evaluation of subcontractors 44

    7.4.2 4.6.3 .... Purchasing data information 45

    7.4.3 4.6.4 .... Verification of purchased product 47

    4.10.2 .... Receiving inspection and testing 47

        4.10.2.1 47

        4.10.2.2 47

        4.10.2.3 47

        4.6.4.1 .... Supplier verification at subcontractor's premises 47

        4.0.4.2 .... Customer verification of subcontracted product 47

7.5 .... Production and service provision 48

    7.5.1 4.9 .... Process Control of production and service provision 48

    4.19 .... Servicing 18

    7.5.2 .... Validation of processes for production and service provision 50

    7.5.3 4.8 .... Product Identification and traceability 51

    7.5.4 4.7 .... Control of Customer supplied product property 53

    7.5.5 .... Preservation of product 54

4.15 .... Handling, storage, packaging, preservation, and delivery 54

    4.15.1 .... General 54

    4.15.2 .... Handling 54

    4.15.3 .... Storage 54

    4.15.4 .... Packaging 54

    4.15.5 .... Preservation 54

    4.15.6 .... Delivery 54

7.6 4.11 .... Control of inspection, monitoring and measuring, and test equipment devices 56

    4.11.1 .... General 56

    4.11.2 .... Control procedure 56

8 4.20 ... Statistical techniques Measurement, analysis and improvement 58

8.1 4.20.1 .... Identification of need General 58

    4.20.2 .... Procedures 58

8.2 .... Monitoring and measurement 59

    8.2.1 .... Customer satisfaction 59

    8.2.2 4.17 .... Internal quality audits 60

    8.2.3 .... Monitoring and measurement of processes 62

    8.2.4 4.10 .... Inspection and testing Monitoring and measurement of product 62

    4.10.1 .... General 62

    4.10.3 .... In-process inspection and testing 62

    4.10.4 .... Final inspection and testing 62

    4.10.5 .... Inspection and test records 63

8.3 4.13 .... Control of nonconforming product 64

    4.13.1 .... General 64

    4.13.2 .... Review and disposition of nonconforming product 64

8.4 .... Analysis of data 66

8.5 .... Improvement 67

    8.5.1 .... Continual improvement 67

    8.5.2 4.14 .... Corrective ~~and preventive~~ action 68

    ~~4.14.1~~ .... ~~General~~ 68

    ~~4.14.2~~ .... ~~Corrective action~~ 68

    8.5.3 ~~4.14.3~~ .... Preventive action 69

Annex A (informative) 71

Annex B (informative) 71

Bibliography 71

Key Words (author originated) 73

Words That Require Definition (author originated) 77

Table of Contents—2000 Version

Page

Foreword v

Acknowledgments vii

Preface.. xxi

Conventions xxiii
    Text conventions xxiii
    Typeface xxiii
    Meaning xxiii
    Footnotes xxiii
    Language xxiii
    Line numbers xxiii
    Order xxiii
    Punctuation xxiii

Introduction.. 1
    0.1 .... General 1
    0.2 .... Process approach 1
    0.3 .... Relationship with ISO 9004 3
    0.4 .... Compatibility with other management systems 3

1 .... Scope 5
    1.1 .... General 5
    1.2 .... Application 5

2 .... Normative reference 6

3 .... Terms and definitions 6

4 .... Quality management system 7
    4.1 .... General requirements 7
    4.2 .... Documentation requirements 10
    4.2.1 .... General 10
    4.2.2 .... Quality manual 13
    4.2.3 .... Control of documents 14
    4.2.4 .... Control of records 16

5 .... Management responsibility 17
    5.1 .... Management commitment 17
    5.2 .... Customer focus 18
    5.3 .... Quality policy 18
    5.4 .... Planning 20
    5.4.1 .... Quality objectives 20
    5.4.2 .... Quality management system planning 20

5.5 ....Responsibility, authority and communication..21
  5.5.1 ....Responsibility and authority 21
  5.5.2 ....Management representative...22
  5.5.3 ....Internal communication..23
5.6 ....Management review 24
  5.6.1 ....General..24
  5.6.2 ....Review input 25
  5.6.3 ....Review output..26

6 .... Resource management 26
6.1 ....Provision of resources..26
6.2 ....Human resources 27
  6.2.1 ....General..27
  6.2.2 ....Competence, awareness and training.................................28
6.3 ....Infrastructure 29
6.4 ....Work environment 29

7 .... Product realization 30
7.1 ....Planning of product realization...30
7.2 ....Customer-related processes..33
  7.2.1 ....Determination of requirements related to the product 33
  7.2.2 ....Review of requirements related to the product....................34
  7.2.3 ....Customer communication..36
7.3 ....Design and development..36
  7.3.1 ....Design and development planning......................................36
  7.3.2 ....Design and development inputs 38
  7.3.3 ....Design and development outputs......................................39
  7.3.4 ....Design and development review..40
  7.3.5 ....Design and development verification..................................41
  7.3.6 ....Design and development validation 42
  7.3.7 ....Control of design and development changes........................43
7.4 ....Purchasing 44
  7.4.1 ....Purchasing process 44
  7.4.2 ....Purchasing information 45
  7.4.3 ....Verification of purchased product 47
7.5 ....Production and service provision..48
  7.5.1 ....Control of production and service provision.........................48
  7.5.2 ....Validation of processes for production and service provision...50
  7.5.3 ....Identification and traceability...51
  7.5.4 ....Customer property 53
  7.5.5 ....Preservation of product 54
7.6 ....Control of monitoring and measuring devices 56

8 .... Measurement, analysis and improvement 58
8.1 ....General...58
8.2 ....Monitoring and measurement..59
  8.2.1 ....Customer satisfaction..59
  8.2.2 ....Internal audit...60
  8.2.3 ....Monitoring and measurement of processes 62
  8.2.4 ....Monitoring and measurement of product 62

8.3..................Control of nonconforming product...64

8.4..................Analysis of data..66

8.5..................Improvement..67

   8.5.1...................Continual improvement...67

   8.5.2...................Corrective action...68

   8.5.3...................Preventive action..69

Annex A (informative)..71

Annex B (informative)..71

Bibliography...71

Key Words (author originated)..73

Words That Require Definition (author originated) 77

Foreword

ISO (the International Organization for Standardization) is a worldwide federation of national standards bodies (ISO member bodies). The work of preparing International Standards is normally carried out through ISO technical committees. Each member body interested in a subject for which a technical committee has been established has the right to be represented on that committee. International organizations, governmental and non-governmental, in liaison with ISO, also take part in the work. ISO collaborates closely with the International Electrotechnical Commission (IEC) on all matters of electrotechnical standardization. The American National Standards Institute (ANSI) is the U.S. member body of ISO. ASQC is the U.S. member of ANSI responsible for quality management and related standards.

International Standards are drafted in accordance with the rules given in the ISO/IEC Directives, Part 3.

Draft International Standards adopted by the technical committees are circulated to the member bodies for voting. Publication as an International Standard requires approval by at least 75% of the member bodies casting a vote.

Attention is drawn to the possibility that some of the elements of this International Standard may be subject of patent rights. ISO shall not be held responsible for identifying any or all such patent rights.

International Standard, ISO 9001 was prepared by Technical Committee ISO/TC 176, *Quality management and quality assurance*, Subcommittee SC 2, *Quality systems.*

This third edition of ISO 9001 cancels and replaces the second edition (ISO 9001:1994) together with ISO 9002:1994 and ISO 9003:1994. It constitutes a technical revision of these documents. Those organizations which have used ISO 9002:1994 and ISO 9003:1994 in the past may use this International Standard by excluding certain requirements in accordance with 1.2.

The title of ISO 9001 has been revised in this edition and no longer includes the term "Quality assurance." This reflects the fact that the quality management system requirements specified in this edition of ISO 9001, in addition to quality assurance of product, also aim to enhance customer satisfaction.

Annexes A and B of this International Standard are for information only.

Preface

The ISO 9001:2000 Auditor's Companion is designed to assist you in either auditing a quality management system or in researching the ANSI/ISO/ASQ Q9001:1994 and 2000. *The Companion* is intended to be a timesaving tool complete with clause-by-clause text of the ISO 9001 standard, reference comparison of the 2000 revisions, guidance notes, and relevant questions for auditing a quality management system.

A word-for-word comparison is made between the ANSI/ISO/ASQ Q9001:1994 and Q9001:2000. The original text is illustrated in normal type with strikeout (line through) used to illustrate any deletions. Redline (shaded) text represents the 2000 additions and/or changes. At a glance you can tell what changes have been made to the ISO 9001 standard. Along with the redline/strikeout text are helpful comments and checklist questions carefully prepared to help with your review of each clause. *The ISO 9001:2000 Auditor's Companion* is designed to help you efficiently perform more effective audits and save valuable time required to update your quality management system to the new requirements. Text within a box in this book is not a part of the ISO 9001 standard. The boxes highlight important points in the standard. See the following example:

Author's Notes

Author's notes are intended to shed light on how the various clauses of the standard are viewed.

Included are comments on whether there is a **change**, a **relaxation**, or a **clarification** introduced in the 2000 version of ISO 9001.

Checklist

Checklist items appear in this area and serve as a convenient reference during the assessment of a facility. The checklist items in *The ISO 9001:2000 Auditor's Companion* reflect the checklist items contained in *The ISO 9001:2000 Audit Kit*.

Another feature of *The ISO 9001:2000 Auditor's Companion* is the line numbering, which appears in the left margin. Line numbering combined with the Key Words and Words That Require Definition at the end of the book are excellent research and communication tools. If a word is unclear or gives you some concern, you may be able to look in the back of this book and find a reference to each place that the word appears in the standard. Thus, light may be shed on this usage of the word by making a quick comparison of how the word is used other places in the standard.

Kent A. Keeney
P.O. Box 905, 533 Henry Street
Huntington, IN 46750
Phone: 219.356.6092, Fax: 219.356.6006
E-mail: kent@hqa.com
Update at Website www.hqa.com

Conventions

Special conventions are used to help you get the most from this book and from auditing a quality management system or in researching the ANSI/ISO/ASQ Q9001–2000.

Text conventions

Various typefaces in this book identify the 1994 and 2000 versions of the ANSI/ISO/ASQ Q9001–2000. These special typefaces include the following:

Typeface	Meaning
~~Strikethrough~~	Text from the 1994 standard which has been deleted or changed in the 2000 version
Shaded	Text in the 2000 version which represents additions and/or changes to the 1994 version.
Normal	Text which is common to both the 1994 and 2000 versions of the standard.

Footnotes

Footnotes show traceability where this is not evident. In some cases, text from the 1994 standard has been moved to a different or new element. The footnotes identify where that text originally appeared (element, paragraph, and sentence, if necessary) in the 1994 standard.

Language

Because this is a comparison of American National Standards, conventional American spelling is used throughout this book, just as it appears in the Standards. Some readers may be used to the British spelling of some words, such as "analyse" vs. "analyze." However, the meaning is in no way affected.

Line numbers

Each line of the standard is numbered in the left margin. These numbers are referenced in the footnotes, the Author's Notes, and the reference sections, "Key Words" and "Words That Require Definition," which appear at the end of this book.

Order

Where possible, the text of the 1994 version precedes the text of the 2000 version. By keeping this in mind, you will be able to more easily compare the 1994 wording to the current, 2000, wording. In the case of alphabetized and numbered lists, the order of the 2000 version is followed.

Punctuation

Capitalization: Occasionally a word appears capitalized in one version and not the other. This is handled by following the capitalization in the 2000 version and shading the letter. This serves to show the reader that a change in capitalization has occurred. For example, the C in Control is shaded below. This indicates that it was not capitalized in the 1994 version, but has been in the 2000 version.

4.5 4.2.3   ~~Document and data~~ Control of documents

Colons: The 1994 version precedes lists with a colon (:). The 2000 version omits the colon. Therefore, we have shown where a colon has been removed by a strikethrough over a colon (~~:~~).

Hyphens: The 1994 version uses hyphens in a number of places whereas the 2000 version does not. For example, the terminology "quality-system" in the 1994 version (notice the use of the hyphen) has been replaced with "quality management system" in the 2000 version (notice the omission of the hyphen). To improve legibility, we have omitted the hyphen when showing the correspondence of the two standards. The chart below shows how we have handled this.

1994 text	4	Quality-system requirements
2000 text	4	Quality management system
Not: (hyphen with strikethrough)	**4**	**Quality-management system ~~requirements~~**
Rather: (hyphen omitted)	**4**	**Quality management system ~~requirements~~**

Introduction

0.1 General

This American National Standard is one of three American National Standards dealing with quality-system requirements that can be used for external quality-assurance purposes. The quality-assurance models, set out in the three American National Standards listed below, represent three distinct forms of quality-system requirements suitable for the purpose of a supplier demonstrating its capability, and for the assessment of the capability of a supplier by external parties.

a) ANSI/ASQC Q9001–1994, *Quality Systems—Model for Quality Assurance in Design, Development, Production, Installation, and Servicing*

— for use when conformance to specified requirements is to be assured by the supplier during design, development, production, installation, and servicing.

b) ANSI/ASQC Q9002–1994, *Quality Systems—Model for Quality Assurance in Production, Installation, and Servicing*

— for use when conformance to specified requirements is to be assured by the supplier during production, installation, and servicing.

c) ANSI/ASQC Q9003–1994, *Quality Systems—Model for Quality Assurance in Final Inspection and Test*

— for use when conformance to specified requirements is to be assured by the supplier solely at final inspection and test.

The adoption of a quality management system should be a strategic decision of an organization. The design and implementation of a an organization's quality management system will be is influenced by the varying needs of an organization, its particular objectives, the products provided, and services supplied, and the processes and specific practices employed and the size and structure of the organization. It is not the intent of this International Standard to imply uniformity in the structure of quality management systems or uniformity of documentation.

It is emphasized that The quality management system requirements specified in this American International National Standard, ANSI/ASQC Q9002–1994, and ANSI/ASQC Q9003–1994 are complementary (not alternative) to the technical (product) specified requirements for products. They specify requirements which determine what elements quality systems have to encompass, but it is not the purpose of these American National Standards to enforce uniformity of quality systems. They are generic and independent of any specific industry or economic sector. Information marked "NOTE" is for guidance in understanding or clarifying the associated requirement.

This International Standard can be used by internal and external parties, including certification bodies, to assess the organization's ability to meet customer, regulatory and the organization's own requirements.

The quality management principles stated in ISO 9000 and ISO 9004 have been taken into consideration during the development of this International Standard.

It is intended that these American National Standards will be adopted in their present form, but on occasions they may need to be tailored by adding or deleting certain quality-system requirements for specific contractual situations. ANSI/ASQC Q9000–1–1994 provides guidance on such tailoring as well as on selection of the appropriate quality-assurance model, *viz.* ANSI/ASQC Q9001–1994, ANSI/ASQC Q9002–1994, or ANSI/ASQC Q9003–1994.

0.2 Process approach

This International Standard promotes the adoption of a process approach when developing, implementing and improving the effectiveness of a quality management system, to enhance customer satisfaction by meeting customer requirements.

For an organization to function effectively, it has to identify and manage numerous linked activities. An activity using resources, and managed in order to enable the transformation of inputs into outputs, can be considered as a process. Often the output from one process directly forms the input to the next.

47 The application of a system of processes within an organization, together with the identification and interac-
48 tions of these processes, and their management, can be referred to as the "process approach."

49 An advantage of the process approach is the ongoing control that it provides over the linkage between the
50 individual processes within the system of processes, as well as over their combination and interaction.

51 When used within a quality management system, such an approach emphasizes the importance of

52 a)   understanding and meeting requirements,

53 b)   the need to consider processes in terms of added value,

54 c)   obtaining results of process performance and effectiveness, and

55 d)   continual improvement of processes based on objective measurement.

56 The model of a process-based quality management system shown in Figure 1 illustrates the process linkages
57 presented in clauses 4 to 8. This illustration shows that customers play a significant role in defining require-
58 ments as inputs. Monitoring of customer satisfaction requires the evaluation of information relating to customer
59 perception as to whether the organization has met the customer requirements. The model shown in Figure 1
60 covers all the requirements of this International Standard, but does not show processes at a detailed level.

61 NOTE: In addition, the methodology known as "Plan-Do-Check-Act" (PDCA) can be applied to all processes.
62 PDCA can be briefly described as follows.

63   Plan: establish the objectives and processes necessary to deliver results in accordance with customer
64   requirements and the organization's policies.

65   Do: implement the processes.

66   Check: monitor and measure processes and product against policies, objectives and requirements for
67   the product and report the results.

68   Act: take actions to continually improve process performance.

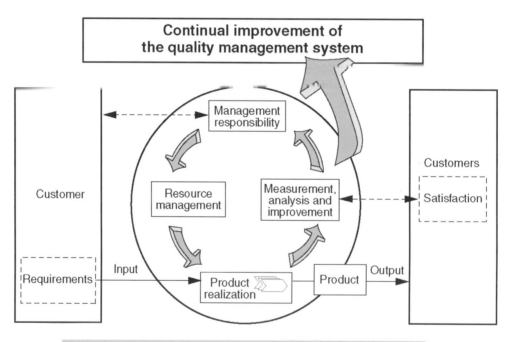

69 **Figure 1 — Model of a process-based quality management system**

Source: ANSI/ISO/ASQ Q9001-2000. Used with permission.

0.3   Relationship with ISO 9004

The present editions of ISO 9001 and ISO 9004 have been developed as a consistent pair of quality management system standards which have been designed to complement each other, but can also be used independ-
ently. Although the two International Standards have different scopes, they have similar structures in order to
assist their application as a consistent pair.

ISO 9001 specifies requirements for a quality management system that can be used for internal application
by organizations, or for certification, or for contractual purposes. It focuses on the effectiveness of the quality
management system in meeting customer requirements.

ISO 9004 gives guidance on a wider range of objectives of a quality management system than does ISO 9001,
particularly for the continual improvement of an organization's overall performance and efficiency, as well as
its effectiveness. ISO 9004 is recommended as a guide for organizations whose top management wishes to
move beyond the requirements of ISO 9001, in pursuit of continual improvement of performance. However,
it is not intended for certification or for contractual purposes.

0.4   Compatibility with other management systems

This International Standard has been aligned with ISO 14001:1996 in order to enhance the compatibility of the
two standards for the benefit of the user community.

This International Standard does not include requirements specific to other management systems, such as
those particular to environmental management, occupational health and safety management, financial management or risk management. However, this International Standard enables an organization to align or integrate its own quality management system with related management system requirements. It is possible for an
organization to adapt its existing management system(s) in order to establish a quality management system
that complies with the requirements of this International Standard.

Author's Notes

The term "aligned," line 84, indicates that the structure of standards ISO 9001:2000 and ISO 14001:1996 is lined
up.

For example, the term "integrate," lines 88 and 89, refers to the practice of merging two systems, such as the quality
management system (QMS) of ISO 9001:2000 and the environmental management system (EMS) of ISO 14001:
1996 into one set of processes and one overall, level-one manual, that includes or makes reference to procedures
for both systems. Typically, both systems are reviewed in the same management review meeting.

1   Scope

1.1   General

This ~~American National~~ International Standard specifies ~~quality system~~ requirements for ~~use where a~~ ~~supplier's capability to design and supply conforming product needs to be demonstrated~~ a quality management system where an organization

a)   needs to demonstrate its ability to consistently provide product that meets customer and applicable regulatory requirements, and

b)   aims to enhance customer satisfaction through the effective application of the system, including processes for continual improvement of the system and the assurance of conformity to customer and applicable regulatory requirements.

NOTE   In this International Standard, the term "product" applies only to the product intended for, or required by, a customer.[1]

~~The requirements specified are aimed primarily at achieving customer satisfaction by preventing noncon-formity at all stages from design through to servicing.~~

~~This American National Standard is applicable in situations when~~

~~a)   design is required and the product requirements are stated principally in performance terms, or they need to be established, and~~

~~b)   confidence in product conformance can be attained by adequate demonstration of a supplier's capa-bilities in design, development, production, installation, and servicing~~

~~NOTE 1   For informative references, see annex A~~

1.2   Application

All requirements of this International Standard are generic and are intended to be applicable to all organizations, regardless of type, size and product provided.

Where any requirement(s) of this International Standard cannot be applied due to the nature of an organization and its product, this can be considered for exclusion.

Where exclusions are made, claims of conformity to this International Standard are not acceptable unless these exclusions are limited to requirements within clause 7, and such exclusions do not affect the organization's ability, or responsibility, to provide product that meets customer and applicable regulatory requirements.

---

1.   Lines 102, 103 were previously NOTE 4 (1994). See lines 147–149.

2 Normative reference

The following ~~standard~~ normative document contains provisions which, through reference in this text, constitute provisions of this ~~American National~~ International Standard. ~~At the time of publication, the edition indicated was valid.~~ For dated references, subsequent amendments to, or revisions of, any of these publications do not apply. However, ~~All standards are subject to revision, and~~ parties to agreements based on this ~~American National~~ International Standard are encouraged to investigate the possibility of applying the most recent edition of the ~~standard~~ normative document indicated below. For undated references, the latest edition of the normative document referred to applies. ~~The American National Standards Institute and~~ Members of ~~IEC~~ ISO and ~~ISO~~ IEC maintain registers of currently valid ~~American National Standards and~~ International Standards.

ISO ~~8402:1994~~ 9000:2000, *Quality management systems ~~and quality assurance~~ — Fundamentals and vocabulary.*

3 Terms and definitions

For the purposes of this ~~American National~~ International Standard, the terms and definitions given in ISO ~~8402~~ 9000 ~~and the following definitions~~ apply.

The following terms, used in this edition of ISO 9001 to describe the supply chain, have been changed to reflect the vocabulary currently used:

supplier ——————> organization ——————> customer

The term "organization" replaces the term "supplier" used in ISO 9001:1994, and refers to the unit to which this International Standard applies. Also, the term "supplier" now replaces the term "subcontractor."

3.1 ~~**product:** Result of activities or processes~~

~~NOTES~~

~~2 A product may include service, hardware, processed materials, software, or a combination thereof.~~

~~3 A product can be tangible (e.g., assemblies or processed materials) or intangible (e.g., knowledge or concepts), or a combination thereof.~~

~~4 For the purposes of this American National Standard, the term "product" applies to the intended product offering only and not to unintended "by-products" affecting the environment. This differs from the definition given in ISO 8402.[1]~~

Throughout the text of this International Standard, wherever the term "product" occurs, it can also mean "service."

3.2 ~~**tender:** Offer made by a supplier in response to an invitation to satisfy a contract award to provide product.~~

3.3 ~~**contract; accepted order:** Agreed requirements between a supplier and customer transmitted by any means.~~

---

1. Lines 147–149 appear under 1.1 in the 2000 version. See lines 102, 103.

156 **4**　　**Quality management system requirements**

157 **4.1**　　**General requirements**[1]

158 The ~~supplier~~ organization shall establish, document, implement, and maintain a quality management
159 system ~~as a means of ensuring that product conforms to specified requirements~~ and continually improve
160 its effectiveness in accordance with the requirements of this International Standard.[2]

Author's Notes

Change—The emphasis shift from conforming product to specified requirements in the 1994 version to continually improving quality management system effectiveness in the 2000 version is consistent with the overall continuous improvement philosophy.

Checklist

A.　In accordance with the requirements of ISO 9001:2000, is our quality management system:
- ❑　Established?
- ❑　Documented?
- ❑　Implemented?
- ❑　Maintained?
- ❑　Continually improving effectiveness?

1.　4.1 "Management Responsibility" (1994) is addressed in 5 (2000).
2.　Lines 158–160 were previously 4.2.1 (1994).

161 The organization shall:

162 a)   identify the processes needed for the quality management system and their application throughout
163   the organization (see 1.2),

164 b)   determine the sequence and interaction of these processes,

165 c)   determine criteria and methods needed to ensure that both the operation and control of these proc-
166   esses are effective,

167 d)   ensure the availability of resources and information necessary to support the operation and monitoring
168   of these processes,

169 e)   monitor, measure and analyze these processes, and

170 f)   implement actions necessary to achieve planned results and continual improvement of these proc-
171   esses.

172 These processes shall be managed by the organization in accordance with the requirements of this
173 International Standard.

174 Where an organization chooses to outsource any process that affects product conformity with require-
175 ments, the organization shall ensure control over such processes. Control of such outsourced processes
176 shall be identified within the quality management system.

177 NOTE   Processes needed for the quality management system referred to above should include pro-
178 cesses for management activities, provision of resources, product realization and measurement

Author's Notes

Change—Lines 161–173 emphasize the process approach. For many organizations this represents an expansion of scope to include the "processes needed for the quality management system" and to further include "their application throughout the organization." Exactly how and to what extent the organization will both identify processes and determine their sequence and interaction will be determined by the size of the organization and the complexity of the processes. Some companies may flowchart all processes while others may take a simple approach relying on travelers, routing information, x-y matrices, process sheets, procedures, work instructions and/or move tickets to define processes and their sequence and interaction.

Lines 174–176 represent a new requirement, to "ensure control" over outsourced processes. Typical outsourced processes might include painting, plating, heat treating, machining, polishing, tooling, and so on. Typical outsourced processes for service organizations might include answering services, mail sorting, packaging, and so on.

Ensuring control can include many degrees or levels of control, such as process design, audits, inspections and/or requiring supplier quality management system registration.

The NOTE, lines 177 and 178, does not represent a mandatory requirement, as noted by the term "should" in place of the mandatory term "shall." The reference to management activities, provision of resources, product realization, and measurement are direct references to sections 5, 6, 7, and 8 of ISO 9001:2000 (see also Figure 1, line 69). Refer to lines 29 and 30 for information on how notes are used in ISO 9001:2000.

Checklist

A. Have we:
- ☐ Identified the processes needed for the quality management system and their application throughout our organization?
- ☐ Determined the sequence and interaction of these processes?
- ☐ Determined criteria and methods needed to ensure both the operation and control of these processes are effective?
- ☐ Ensured the availability of resources and information necessary to support the operation and monitoring of these processes?
- ☐ Monitored, measured, and analyzed these processes?
- ☐ Implemented action(s) necessary to achieve planned results and continual improvement of these processes?
B. Have we managed these processes in accordance with the requirements of ISO 9001:2000?
C. Where we have chosen to outsource any process that affects product conformity with requirements, have we ensured control over the processes?
D. Is the control of the outsourced processes identified within our quality management system?

179 **4.2** ~~Quality system~~ **Documentation requirements**

180 **4.2.1** **General**

181 ~~**4.2.2**~~ ~~**Quality-system procedures**~~

182 The ~~supplier~~ quality management system documentation shall include

183 a) documented statements of a quality policy and quality objectives,

184 b) ~~prepare~~ a quality manual, ~~covering the requirements of this American National Standard.~~[1]

185 c) ~~a) prepare~~ documented procedures ~~consistent with the requirements of this American National~~
186 ~~Standard and the supplier's stated quality policy, and~~ required by this International Standard,

187 d) ~~b) effectively implement the quality system and its documented procedures.~~ documents needed by
188 the organization to ensure the effective planning, operation and control of its processes, and

189 e) records required by this International Standard (see 4.2.4).

Author's Notes

Clearly, the *amount* of documentation may vary. For example, increasing the amount of training may significantly reduce either the number of documented procedures and work instructions required or the level of detail required within these documents.

Note the degree of documentation ultimately depends on methods used, organization size, processes and their interaction, and personnel competence. See note 2, lines 194–199.

Change—You probably will notice little change in the way registrars review documented procedures and manuals. However, the amount of documentation required has been substantially reduced. For example, the year 2000 version requires a minimum of six procedures, while the 1994 version required almost one for each of the previous 4.1 thru 4.20 elements. The emphasis on the intent of the documentation, lines 187 and 188, item d, has shifted in the year 2000 version, from "requiring documentation to effectively implement the quality management system" to now emphasize "ensuring effective planning, operation, and control of the organization's processes." This further emphasizes the process approach.

Particularly for small businesses and service organizations, the structure of the procedures and the amount of documentation will vary depending on a number of factors that are the responsibility of your organization to determine. There is not one standardized approach to be used by all organizations.

Change—Line 183, item a, the reference to a documented statement of quality policy is not new. However, the reference to quality objectives is new and may require some clarification of those quality objectives; see lines 183, 262, 276, 281, 282, 283, 288, 325, 360, 380, and 859 for each mention of quality objectives in the 2000 version.

Checklist

A. Does our quality management system documentation include:
- ❑ A documented statement of a quality policy?
- ❑ A documented statement of quality objectives?
- ❑ A quality manual?
- ❑ Documented procedures required by ISO 9001:2000?
- ❑ Documents that we need to ensure the effective planning, operation, and control of our processes?
- ❑ Records required by ISO 9001:2000? (see 4.2.4)

---

1. Line 184 was previously 4.2.1 paragraph 1, sentence 2 (1994).

190 ~~NOTE 7~~ ~~Documented procedures may make reference to work instructions that define how an activity~~
191 ~~is performed.~~

192 NOTE 1   Where the term "documented procedure" appears within this International Standard, this
193 means that the procedure is established, documented, implemented and maintained.

194 NOTE 2   ~~For the purposes of this American National Standard, the range and detail~~ The extent of the
195 ~~procedures that form part of the~~ quality management system documentation can differ from one organiza-
196 tion to another ~~depend on~~ due to

197 a)   ~~the~~ size of organization and type of activities,

198 b)   the complexity of ~~the work, the methods used,~~ processes and their interactions, and

199 c)   the ~~skills and training needed by~~ competence of personnel ~~involved in~~ carrying out the activity.

200 ~~NOTE 15~~ 3   ~~Documents~~ and data The documentation can be in ~~the~~ any form ~~of any~~ or type of ~~media,~~
201 ~~such as hard copy or electronic media~~ medium.[1]

Author's Notes

The minimum number of required procedures is reduced to six in the year 2000 version. They include:
- ❑   Control of Documents, 4.2.3, lines 218–241
- ❑   Control of Records, 4.2.4, lines 247–250
- ❑   Internal Audits, 8.2.2, lines 764 and 765
- ❑   Control of Nonconforming Product, 8.3, lines 819–822
- ❑   Corrective Action, 8.5.2, lines 872–882
- ❑   Preventive Action, 8.5.3, lines 886–898

Clarification—NOTE 1, lines 192 and 193, is essentially a definition of a "documented procedure." The fact that the procedure is established, documented, implemented, and maintained is consistent with the manner that procedures were implemented and audited in the 1994 version.

Checklist

No corresponding checklist items exist for NOTES. As indicated in line 29, "information marked "NOTE" is for guidance in understanding or clarifying the associated requirement."

---

1.   Lines 201, 202 were previously NOTE 15 under 4.5 "Document and Data Control" (1994).

202 **4.2.2   Quality manual**

203 The ~~supplier~~ organization shall ~~prepare~~ establish and maintain a quality manual ~~covering the requirements~~
204 ~~of this American National Standard~~ that includes

205 a)   the scope of the quality management system, including details of and justification for any exclusions
206   (see 1.2),

207 b)   ~~The quality manual shall include or make reference to~~ the ~~quality system~~ documented procedures
208   established for the quality management system, or reference to them, and

209 c)   ~~outline the structure of the documentation used in~~ a description of the interaction between the proc-
210   ~~esses~~ of the quality management system.

211 ~~NOTE 6   Guidance on quality manuals is given in ISO 10013.~~

Author's Notes

A quality manual is required. The quality manual must include or make reference to procedures and outline the structure of the documentation. This may be accomplished in a variety of ways: by a document map, by listing procedures in each section of the manual, by numbering the procedures to correspond to certain sections of the manual, and so on.

The manual can either contain considerable detail or be very concise and guide you into the rest of the documented quality management system.

Clarification—Line 203 is a clarification of previously existing requirements and simply restates that a quality manual is required and it is to be maintained.

Change—Item a, line 205, states that a scope statement is now required in the quality manual. The scope statement defines the boundary of the quality management system, describing inclusions and perhaps more importantly, "permissible exclusions." Typical exclusions are design and development (7.3) and customer property (7.5.4). Some may also want to exclude the service provision portion of 7.5.

Item b, lines 207 and 208, is a clarification and does not represent a real change. A documentation map, listing relevant procedures in each section of the quality manual and/or using a significant numbering system on procedures, can accomplish this also.

Change—Item c, lines 209 and 210, is a change that may be easy for some companies and may involve considerable work for others, depending on the size and complexity of the organization. For a less complex company, Figure 1, line 69, of this document along with any quality management system documentation may be sufficient to describe the "interaction between processes." Larger or more complex companies may find it a value add to use more detailed descriptions, such as flowcharts, x-y matrices, travelers, routing sheets, move tickets, work orders, and so on.

Reference to ISO 10013 as a guidance document for preparing quality manuals has been deleted.

Checklist

A.   Has a quality manual been established and maintained that includes:
- ❑   The scope of the quality management system, including details of and justification for any exclusions?
- ❑   Documented procedures established for the quality management system or reference to them?
- ❑   A description of the interaction between the processes of the quality management system?

212 **4.2.3 4.5** ~~Document and data~~ Control of documents

213 **~~4.5.1~~** **~~General~~**

214 **~~4.5.2~~** **~~Document and data approval and issue~~**

215 **~~4.5.3~~** **~~Document and data changes~~**

216 Documents required by the quality management system shall be controlled. Records are a special type
217 of document and shall be controlled according to the requirements given in 4.2.4.

218 A ~~master list or equivalent document-control~~ documented procedure ~~identifying the current revision status~~
219 ~~of documents~~ shall be established ~~and be readily available to preclude the use of invalid and/or obsolete~~
220 ~~documents.~~ to define the controls needed

221 ~~This control shall ensure that:~~

222 a) ~~The documents and data shall be reviewed and approved for adequacy by authorized personnel~~ to
223 approve documents for adequacy ~~prior to issue,~~[1]

224 b) ~~Changes to documents and data shall be reviewed and approved by the same functions/organizations~~
225 ~~that performed the original review and approval, unless specifically designated otherwise. The desig-~~
226 ~~nated functions/organizations shall have access to pertinent background information upon which to~~
227 ~~base their review and approval.~~ to review and update as necessary and re-approve documents,[2]

228 c) ~~Where practicable, the nature of the change shall be identified in the document or the appropriate~~
229 ~~attachments.~~ to ensure that changes and the current revision status of documents are identified,[3]

230 d) ~~a) the pertinent issues of appropriate~~ to ensure that relevant versions of applicable documents are
231 available at ~~all locations where operations essential to the effective functioning of the quality system~~
232 ~~are performed;~~ points of use,

233 e) to ensure that documents remain legible and readily identifiable,

234 f) ~~The supplier shall establish and maintain documented procedures to control all documents and data~~
235 ~~that relate to the requirements of this American National Standard including, to the extent applicable,~~
236 to ensure that documents of external origin ~~such as standards and customer drawings.~~ are identified
237 and their distribution controlled, and[4]

238 g) ~~b) invalid and/or~~ to prevent the unintended use of obsolete documents ~~are promptly removed from~~
239 ~~all points of issue or use, or otherwise assured against unintended use; c) any obsolete documents~~
240 ~~retained for legal and/or knowledge-preservation purposes are suitably identified.~~ and to apply suitable
241 identification to them if they are retained for any purpose.[5]

---

1. Lines 223 and 224 were previously 4.5.2, paragraph 1, sentence 1 (1994).
2. Lines 225–228 were previously 4.5.3, paragraph 1 (1994).
3. Lines 229 and 230 were previously 4.5.3, paragraph 2 (1994).
4. Lines 235–237 were previously 4.5.1, paragraph 1 (1994).
5. Lines 239–241 were previously 4.5.2.b and 4.5.2.c (1994).

Author's Notes

Clarification

Lines 216 and 217 add a reference to records (formerly quality records) as a "special type of document." This does not change the common distinction that many records are simply documents (forms are an example) with information added to the form to "record" an event.

Clarification—Lines 218–220 refer to NOTE 1, lines 192 and 193. As in the 1994 version, documented procedures must be established to identify key documents and to ensure that they are suitably controlled. Standards of external origin may represent a problem for some companies. For example, will the 1994 version of ISO 9001 still be around after the 2000 version is issued? What will be used during internal audits? May photocopies of these standards be made?

The deletion of the term "where practicable" in line 228 is a change to eliminate the option of not identifying the change. Item c, lines 228 and 229, does not preclude the use of a separate document to identify the changes.

Item b might include contracts, drawings, inspection and test instructions, manuals, procedures, purchase orders, specifications, and training records. It is still possible to allow handwritten changes to documents provided that you have a system for dealing with this. The system (occasionally called a redline instruction) should designate who can make such changes, for how long, and the follow-up activity to formalize the change

Item g indicates obsolete documents may be readily accessible provided that the documents are clearly marked. The criteria here is: Will someone mistakenly use the obsolete document for performing quality work?

Clarification—Items e, f, and g do not represent a change of intent.

NOTE 15 in the 1994 version appears as NOTE 3, lines 200 and 201, and again stipulates that "documentation can be in any form or type of medium." Note that each form of media may pose unique document control challenges.

The following three items should be addressed:
- ❑ Identify documents to control
- ❑ Demonstrate control by issue dates, revision status, approvals, master lists, and so on
- ❑ Establish a process for document issue and removal

Checklist

A. Do we control documents required by the quality management system?
B. Do we control records according to the requirements given in 4.2.4? (Records are a special type of document)
C. Have we established a documented procedure to define the controls needed to:
- ❑ Approve documents for adequacy prior to issue?
- ❑ Review and update as necessary and re-approve documents?
- ❑ Ensure that changes and the current revision status of documents are identified?
- ❑ Ensure that relevant versions of applicable documents are available at points of use?
- ❑ Ensure that documents remain legible and readily identifiable?
- ❑ Ensure that documents of external origin are identified and their distribution controlled?
- ❑ Prevent the unintended use of obsolete documents?
- ❑ Apply suitable identification to them if they are retained for any purpose?

242 **4.2.4** 4.16   **Control of quality records**

243 Quality Records shall be established and maintained to demonstrate conformance provide evidence of
244 conformity to specified requirements and of the effective operation of the quality management system.[1]
245 All quality Records shall be remain legible, and shall be stored and retained in such a way that they are
246 readily identifiable and retrievable in facilities that provide a suitable environment to prevent damage or
247 deterioration and to prevent loss.[2] A The supplier shall establish and maintain documented procedures
248 shall be established to define the controls needed for the identification, collection, indexing, access, filing,
249 storage, maintenance, protection, retrieval, retention time and disposition of quality records.[3]

250 Pertinent quality records from the subcontractor shall be an element of these data.

251 Retention times of quality records shall be established and recorded. Where agreed contractually, quality
252 records shall be made available for evaluation by the customer or the customer's representative for an
253 agreed period.

254 NOTE 19   Records may be in the form of any type of media, such as hard copy or electronic media.

Author's Notes

Relaxation—Lines 242–254 represent a relaxation of record control requirements. A record system now contains six elements compared to eight elements (nine if you count retention time) under the 1994 version. Be careful about making blanket statements, such as, "All records will be retained for three years." Training records should be retained for as long as an individual remains at a given company or plant location.

Records typically indicate conformance to requirements rather than achievement of quality. The intent of this section remains unchanged. The organization is now required to maintain procedures or a single procedure addressing identification, storage, protection, retrieval, retention time, and disposition or disposal of records.

It should be obvious that if a record is "demonstrating conformance" the record will identify how that conformance is demonstrated.

Compare "retention time" in lines 249 and 251.

Minimum required records are identified by "(see 4.2.4)" throughout the 2000 version in lines 189, 362, 392, 470, 518, 530, 548, 623, 765, 838, 881, and 897.

Checklist

A. Are records established and maintained to provide evidence of:
    ❏ Production service conformity to requirements?
    ❏ The effective operation of our quality management system?
B. Are records:
    ❏ Legible?
    ❏ Readily identifiable?
    ❏ Retrievable?
C. Have we established a documented procedure to define controls needed for records:
    ❏ Identification?
    ❏ Storage?
    ❏ Protection?
    ❏ Retrieval?
    ❏ Retention time?
    ❏ Disposition or disposal?

---

1. Lines 244–245 were previously 4.16, paragraph 2, sentence 1 (1994).
2. Lines 245–248 were previously 4.16, paragraph 3, sentence 1 (1994).
3. Lines 248–250 were previously 4.16, paragraph 1 (1994).

255 **5 4.1   Management responsibility**

256 **5.1   Management commitment**

257 Top management shall provide evidence of its commitment to the development and implementation of
258 the quality management system and continually improving its effectiveness by

259 a)   communicating to the organization the importance of meeting customer as well as statutory and
260   regulatory requirements,

261 b)   establishing the quality policy,

262 c)   ensuring that quality objectives are established,

263 d)   conducting management reviews, and

264 e)   ensuring the availability of resources.

Author's Notes

Change—Lines 257 and 258 represent a shift in focus from presuming that management is committed to improving the quality management system (QMS) to now requiring *evidence* of that commitment.

Items a–e, lines 259–264, define the evidence that an auditor must investigate to determine compliance. Items b, d, and e are not new. Item e was formerly 4.1.2.2 in the 1994 version. In ISO 9001:2000, however, a and c are new.

Item a is typically accomplished by informational meetings, posters, information boards, performance review processes, company newsletters, new employee orientation, and so on. Statutory and regulatory requirements will differ depending on the industry and the market that the product will go into.

Compare 5.1e in the 2000 version with 4.1.2.2 Resources in the 1994 version:
"The organization shall identify resource requirements and provide adequate resources, including the assignment of trained personnel (see 4.18), for management, performance of work, and verification activities including internal quality audits."

Compare 5.1e in the 2000 version with 4.2.1 Quality System General in the 1994 version:
"The organization shall establish, document, and maintain a quality system as a means of ensuring that product conforms to specified requirements."

Checklist

A.   Has our top management provided evidence of its commitment to the development and implementation of the quality management system and continually improved its effectiveness by:
- ❏   Communicating to our organization the importance of meeting customer as well as statutory and regulatory requirements?
- ❏   Establishing the quality policy?
- ❏   Ensuring that quality objectives are established?
- ❏   Conducting management reviews?
- ❏   Ensuring the availability of resources?

265 **5.2 Customer focus**

266 Top management shall ensure that customer requirements are determined and are met with the aim of
267 enhancing customer satisfaction (see 7.2.1 and 8.2.1).

Author's Notes

Customer focus and 7.2.1 "Determination of requirements related to the product" most closely parallel contract review 4.3.2 in the 1994 version. Here the activity of customer focus includes understanding the customer requirements to the extent that they are adequately defined and agreed to. Determining customer requirements and verifying the organization's capability to meet these requirements is an essential element.

Change—Lines 266 and 267 represent a change from simply defining and meeting requirements in the 1994 version to actually making top management accountable to see that processes are in place to go beyond just meeting. That is, top management should look to comparing those requirements to customer needs and expectations and ensuring processes "enhance" customer satisfaction. Customer requirements, line 266, are addressed in 7.2.1 and 7.2.2 of the 2000 version. See lines 957 and 1037.

Checklist

A. Does our top management ensure that customer requirements are:
   - ❏ Determined?
   - ❏ Met and aimed at enhancing customer satisfaction?
     (see 7.2.1 and 8.2.1)

---

268 **5.3 4.1.1 Quality policy**

269 ~~The supplier's~~ Top management ~~with executive responsibility shall define and document its policy for~~
270 ~~quality, including objectives for quality and its commitment to quality. The quality policy shall be relevant~~
271 ~~to the supplier's organizational goals and the expectations and needs of its customers. The supplier~~ shall
272 ensure that ~~this~~ the quality policy

273 a) is appropriate to the purpose of the organization,

274 b) includes a commitment to comply with requirements and continually improve the effectiveness of the
275 quality management system,

276 c) provides a framework for establishing and reviewing quality objectives,

277 d) is communicated and understood, ~~implemented, and maintained at all levels of~~ within the organiza-
278 tion, and

279 e) is reviewed for continuing suitability.

18

Author's Notes

Change—Item a, line 273, is a change from emphasizing goals to now concentrating on requiring the quality policy to link to the organization's purpose.

Item b, lines 274 and 275, is a change consistent with an overall emphasis throughout the 2000 version to continually improve the effectiveness of the quality management system. This improvement links nicely with the change described in item c, line 276, which refers to quality objectives (see 5.4.1).

Most companies transitioning from the 1994 version to the 2000 version will update their quality policy to include item b, line 274 and 275.

Clarification—Item d, lines 277 and 278, is a clarification. Be certain that new hires, contract employees, and temporary employees know where the quality policy is and that they understand it.

Many companies include a brief explanation of the quality policy in the employee orientation training for each new, contract, and/or temporary employee. It is clear that top management of the organization must define the quality policy. Objectives for and commitment to quality are included. The term "top management" is used now throughout the standard to replace the term "management with executive responsibility." The reason for this is that "top management" is a phrase that will more easily and accurately translate into various languages.

The intent is to encourage the organization to have a policy unique to its goals and customer goals instead of a generic, off-the-shelf policy. The documented quality policy must be known and understood by all employees.

Change—Item e, line 279, now requires a review of the quality policy for continuing suitability. Typically, this review occurs in management review annually. However, the standard does not specifically state or imply a predetermined interval. Some companies may link quality policy review with major changes in the quality management system or changes in business sector.

The quality policy should be:
- ❑ Easily understood
- ❑ Relevant
- ❑ Ambitious (goals), yet realistic and attainable
- ❑ Appropriate for its goals
- ❑ Appropriate for its customers
- ❑ Understood by all

Checklist

A. Has our top management ensured that the quality policy:
- ❑ Is appropriate to the purpose of the organization?
- ❑ Includes a commitment to comply with requirements and continually improve the effectiveness of the quality management system?
- ❑ Provides a framework for establishing and reviewing quality objectives?
- ❑ Is communicated and understood within the organization?
- ❑ Is reviewed for continuing suitability?

280 **5.4   Planning**

281 **5.4.1   Quality objectives**

282 Top management shall ensure that quality objectives, including those needed to meet requirements for
283 product [see 7.1 a], are established at relevant functions and levels within the organization. The quality
284 objectives shall be measurable and consistent with the quality policy.

Author's Notes

Change—Lines 282–284 describe quality objectives. These objectives "shall be measurable." Typical objectives may include key measurables, such as productivity, rework, concessions, scrap, parts per million (PPM), defect rate, and so on. "Quality objectives" appear on lines 183, 262, 276, 282, 283, 288, 325, 360, 380, and 859.

Checklist

A.   Has our top management ensured that quality objectives, including those needed to meet requirements for product [see 7.1a)] have been established at relevant functions and levels within our organization?
B.   Are the quality objectives measurable and consistent with the quality policy?

---

285 **5.4.2   Quality management system planning**[1]

286 Top management shall ensure that

287 a)   the planning of the quality management system is carried out in order to meet the requirements given
288   in 4.1, as well as the quality objectives, and

289 b)   the integrity of the quality management system is maintained when changes to the quality manage-
290   ment system are planned and implemented.

Author's Notes

Change—Lines 285–290 correspond to only a portion of what used to be called quality planning in the 1994 version. See 7.1 of the 2000 version for "planning of product realization." Although quality management system planning is somewhat addressed in 4.2.3 Quality Planning, ISO 9001(1994), the emphasis here is on the proactive involvement of top management.

An auditor will look for the existence of an actual planning process and an actual change process, such as a change notice process (ECN, MCN, PCN, and so on) to verify that this requirement is being met.

Checklist

A.   Has our top management ensured that:
  ❑   The planning of the quality management system is carried out in order to meet requirements given in 4.1, as well as the quality objectives?
  ❑   The integrity of the quality management system is maintained when changes to the quality manage-ment system are planned and implemented?

---

1.   Line 286, 4.2.3 "Quality Planning" (1994) is addressed in 7.1 (2000).

291 **5.5** 4.1.2   ~~Organization~~ Responsibility, authority and communication

292 **5.5.1** ~~4.1.2.1~~   **Responsibility and authority**

293 ~~The responsibility, authority, and the~~ Top management shall ensure that the responsibilities and authori-
294 ~~ties~~ ~~interrelation of personnel who manage, perform, and verify work affecting quality shall be~~ are defined
295 and ~~documented,~~ communicated within the organization ~~particularly for personnel who need the organiza-~~
296 ~~tional freedom and authority to:~~

297 ~~a)~~ ~~initiate action to prevent the occurrence of any nonconformities relating to product, process, and~~
298   ~~quality system;~~

299 ~~b)~~ ~~identify and record any problems relating to the product, process, and quality system;~~

300 ~~c)~~ ~~initiate, recommend, or provide solutions through designated channels;~~

301 ~~d)~~ ~~verify the implementation of solutions;~~

302 ~~e)~~ ~~control further processing, delivery, or installation of nonconforming product until the deficiency or~~
303 ~~unsatisfactory condition has been corrected.~~

Author's Notes

Relaxation—There are a number of ways to accomplish this. This does not mean that job descriptions must be written for every employee, although that may be a good way of communicating responsibility and authority. For example, in addition to job descriptions; flowcharts, organization charts, and documented procedures defining authority represent a partial list of means of potentially satisfying the requirement. Choose the method(s) best suited to add value to your organization's quality management system.

Clarification—Line 294, the apparent limitation of "those whose work affects quality," is now deleted.

Note the definite shift in emphasis away from requiring "documented procedures." This theme of de-emphasizing documentation is apparent throughout the 2000 version. The requirement is to simply communicate this information.

Checklist

A. Has our top management ensured that the responsibilities and authorities are defined and communicated within our organization?

---

304 **5.5.2** ~~4.1.2.3~~ **Management representative**

305 ~~The supplier's~~ Top management ~~with executive responsibility~~ shall appoint a member of ~~the supplier's own~~
306 management who, irrespective of other responsibilities, shall have ~~defined~~ responsibility and authority ~~for~~
307 that includes

308 a) ensuring that ~~a~~ processes needed for the quality management system ~~is~~ are established, imple-
309   mented, and maintained, ~~in accordance with this American National Standard, and~~

310 b) reporting to top management on the performance of the quality management system ~~to the supplier's~~
311   ~~management for review and as a basis~~ and any need for improvement, ~~and~~ ~~of the quality system.~~

312 c) ensuring the promotion of awareness of customer requirements throughout the organization.

313 NOTE ~~5~~   The responsibility of a management representative ~~may also~~ can include liaison with external
314 parties on matters relating to the ~~supplier's~~ quality management system.

Author's Notes

The management representative must be a member of management. Reporting on the performance of the quality management system can be recorded in management review meeting minutes. Management review is a logical place to report on quality management system performance and identify any need for improvement. Some companies fall down here by not empowering the management representative with sufficient authority to get the job done. Since the management representative must be a member of management, the term *management* must be defined. Does management include certain levels or pay grades, or does it include certain titles? Decide and define. Changes in other clauses of the 2000 version may affect the management representative's report to top management (item c). For example, 8.4 Analysis of data, 8.5 Improvement, 5.2 Customer focus, and 5.6.2 Review input could be considered in the report to management.

Change—The management representative has the *responsibility* and authority for making sure that the processes for the quality management system are established, implemented, and maintained. Management is now allowed to delegate this "responsibility."

Item c, line 312, "ensuring the promotion of awareness of customer requirements throughout the organization," is a new requirement. See also lines 43, 59, 63, 77, 266, 312, 339, 348, 432 and 749 for the term "customer requirements." Your definition of customer requirements will determine how you promote awareness. For example, if you limit the definition to just part specifications, then drawings and control plans may be sufficient.

Checklist

A. Has our top management appointed a member of management as the management representative?
B. Does the management representative, irrespective of other responsibilities, have responsibility and authority that includes:
   - ❑ Ensuring that processes needed for the quality management system are established, implemented, and maintained?
   - ❑ Reporting to top management on the performance of the quality management system and any need for improvement?
   - ❑ Ensuring the promotion of awareness of customer requirements throughout the organization?

315 **5.5.3**   **Internal communication**

316 Top management shall ensure that appropriate communication processes are established within the
317 organization and that communication takes places regarding the effectiveness of the quality management
318 system.

Author's Notes

Change—This is a new clause and may be accomplished in a number of ways. Top management might post key measurables in the form of graphs or trend charts. Facility awareness meetings, presentations, newsletters, and/or posters are all means that may facilitate this communication.

Checklist

A.   Has our top management ensured that
- ❑ Appropriate communication processes are established within our organization?
- ❑ Communication takes place regarding the effectiveness of the quality management system?

---

319 **5.6** 4.1.3   **Management review**

320 **5.6.1**   **General**

321 ~~The supplier's~~ Top management ~~with executive responsibility~~ shall review the organization's quality
322 management system, at ~~defined~~ planned intervals, ~~sufficient~~ to ensure its continuing suitability, adequacy
323 and effectiveness. ~~in satisfying the requirements of this American National Standard and the supplier's~~
324 ~~stated~~ This review shall include assessing opportunities for improvement and the need for changes to the
325 quality management system, including the quality policy and quality objectives. ~~(see 4.1.1).~~

326 Records ~~of such~~ from management reviews shall be maintained (see ~~4.16~~ 4.2.4).

Author's Notes

Clarification—This clause requires top management to review the effectiveness, suitability, and *adequacy* of the quality management system and take appropriate action. Internal auditors and others might provide input into this review, but it must be top management who decides how well the quality objectives and quality policy are being met. Meaningful improvement of the quality management system is directed from this review. Although a focus on efficiency is not required by the standard (the standard contains minimum requirements), the degree to which efficiency is emphasized tends to trigger management's meaningful involvement. How far apart the planned intervals should be depends a lot on how well the quality management system is doing, the maturity of the system, and planned improvement changes to achieve quality objectives. Initially, schedule frequent reviews to monitor the system closely. As the program matures, subsequent management reviews may be spaced further apart. These reviews should be proactive. Although the frequency is not prescribed and annual reviews are common practice, seriously question the meaningfulness of the reviews if they occur less frequently than once a quarter. It is significant that management review is now to be performed by the organization's top management. Top management must be concerned with the total system, not just the results of audits. Management reviews must focus on the effectiveness of the entire system by comparing performance data with quality objectives and determining appropriate action, including actually changing the quality policy and quality objectives. New wording very closely links the quality policy to the quality objectives.

Change—The deletion of line 323 and the addition of lines 324 and 325 highlight a basic shift in focus from "satisfying requirements" to constantly seeking opportunities for improvement and initiating change.

The change from "defined" intervals to "planned" intervals indicates that intervals are determined by strategy and forethought rather than arbitrarily defaulting to an interval, such as yearly.

Checklist

A. Does our top management review our quality management system? Is this review at planned intervals to ensure its continuing:
    - ❑ Suitability?
    - ❑ Adequacy?
    - ❑ Effectiveness?
B. Does our management review include assessing opportunities for improvement?
C. Does our management review include assessing the need for changes to the quality management system, including the quality policy and quality objectives?
D. Are records from management reviews maintained? (see 4.2.4)

327 **5.6.2   Review input**

328 The input to management review shall include information on

329 a)   results of audits,

330 b)   customer feedback,

331 c)   process performance and product conformity,

332 d)   status of preventive and corrective actions,

333 e)   follow-up actions from previous management reviews,

334 f)   changes that could affect the quality management system, and

335 g)   recommendations for improvement.

Author's Notes

Change—NOTE 20 under 4.17 in the 1994 version, lines 773 and 775, now appears as lines 328 and 329. It is a shall statement in the 2000 version, however, it was worded like a shall statement in the NOTE in the 1994 version.

Clause 5.6.2 is all new, representing what many will consider a minimum agenda for management reviews. The emphasis is that data from items a through g are reviewed and that management review is audited as a process. Since management review is a process, it must have the above inputs as a minimum and the outputs will be corresponding action items, followed by the appropriate follow-up action as indicated in item e of clause 5.6.2 and as shown in clause 5.6.3.

Checklist

A.   Do inputs to management review include information on:
- ❑   Results of audits?
- ❑   Customer feedback?
- ❑   Process performance and product conformity?
- ❑   Status of preventive and corrective actions?
- ❑   Follow up actions from previous management reviews?
- ❑   Changes that could affect the quality management system?
- ❑   Recommendations for Improvement?

336 **5.6.3**   **Review output**

337 The output from the management review shall include any decisions and actions related to

338 a)   improvement of the effectiveness of the quality management system and its processes,

339 b)   improvement of product related to customer requirements, and

340 c)   resource needs.

Author's Notes

Change—Lines 336–340 represent a shift in focus, particularly in item a, which is the improvement of effectiveness of the quality management system and its processes. Reference to "its processes. . ." in line 338 may be applied to the processes outlined in Figure 1 that reference sections 5, 6, 7, and 8 of the 2000 version.

Item b, line 339, represents a change. While implied in the 1994 version, the actual "improvement of product related customer requirements" was not specifically addressed in the 1994 version. Resource needs, item c, line 340, links to 6.1, Provision of resources, in the 2000 version.

Checklist

A.   Do outputs from the management review include any decisions and actions related to:
   ❑   Improvement of the effectiveness of the quality management system and its processes?
   ❑   Improvement of product related to customer requirements?
   ❑   Resource needs?

---

341 **6**   **Resource management**

342 **6.1 4.1.2.2**   **Provision of resources**

343 The ~~supplier~~ organization shall ~~identify resource requirements~~ determine and provide ~~adequate~~ the
344 resources needed ~~including the assignment of trained personnel (see 4.18), for management, perform-~~
345 ~~ance of work, and verification activities including internal quality audits.~~

346 a)   to implement and maintain the quality management system and continually improve its effectiveness,
347   and

348 b)   to enhance customer satisfaction by meeting customer requirements.

Author's Notes

Change—Resource requirements, although often reviewed as a part of annual budgets, are also reviewed during management review, clause 5.6.3c, to satisfy the standard. The organization's management must now decide what resources are necessary for meeting customer requirements, not just requirements for the quality management system. Meeting customer requirements now includes maintaining the quality management system (QMS) as well as continually improving its effectiveness.

Checklist

A.   Have we determined and provided the resources needed to:
   ❑   Implement and maintain the quality management system and continually improve its effectiveness?
   ❑   Enhance customer satisfaction by meeting customer requirements?

349 **6.2   Human resources**

350 **6.2.1   General**

351 Personnel performing ~~specific assigned tasks~~ work affecting product quality shall be ~~qualified~~ competent
352 on the basis of appropriate education, training, skills and/~~or~~ experience~~, as required~~.[1]

Author's Notes

Change—Lines 351 and 352 shift the emphasis from being "qualified" to now being "competent." Except for the addition of "skills," the assessment of "competence" in the 2000 version is the same as the assessment of "qualified" in the 1994 version. Skills may be defined in job description, testing, periodic evaluations, and so on.

4.2.3b Quality Planning (1994) "The supplier *shall give consideration* to the identification and acquisition of any skills that may be needed to achieve the required quality."

Checklist

A.   Are personnel performing work affecting product quality competent on the basis of appropriate:
   ❑   Education?
   ❑   Training?
   ❑   Skills?
   ❑   Experience?

---

1.   Lines 352 and 353 were previously 4.18, sentence 2 (1994).

| 353 | **6.2.2** 4.18 | **Competence, awareness and training** |

354 The ~~supplier~~ organization shall ~~establish and maintain documented procedures for~~

355 a) ~~identifying training needs~~ determine the necessary competence ~~and provide~~ for ~~the training of all~~
356   personnel performing ~~activities~~ work affecting product quality,

357 b) provide training or take other actions to satisfy these needs,

358 c) evaluate the effectiveness of the actions taken,

359 d) ensure that its personnel are aware of the relevance and importance of their activities and how they
360   contribute to the achievement of the quality objectives, and

361 e) maintain appropriate records of education, training, ~~shall be maintained (see 4.16).~~ skills and experi-
362   ence (see 4.2.4).

Author's Notes

Change—Auditing of competence, awareness, and training will result in a change such that a process for determining competency must be established. Organizations may do this in a number of ways, for example, job descriptions, job profiles, performance reviews, skill assessments, testing, and so on. Auditing the training function is very straight forward and can be performed in three distinct phases or steps.

- ❑ Are training requirements specified?
- ❑ Was the training provided or has it been scheduled?
- ❑ Where are the records of these activities?

In addition to the above 3 items, was the training effective?

Although subtle, item c requires evaluating the effectiveness of actions taken, including training. Training effectiveness can be evaluated in a number of ways including pretest/post test, job performance, return on investment, participant surveys, and so on. Training effectiveness is often evaluated on both short and long term basis.

Change—Clause 6.2.2d, line 359, requires creating awareness of relevance and importance of their activities and how they contribute toward achieving quality objectives.

Checklist

A. Have we:
- ❑ Determined the necessary competence for personnel performing work affecting product quality?
- ❑ Provided training or taken other actions to satisfy these needs?
- ❑ Evaluated the effectiveness of the actions taken?
- ❑ Ensured that our personnel are aware of the relevance and importance of their activities and how they contribute to the achievement of the quality objectives?
- ❑ Maintained appropriate records of education, training, skills, and experience? (see 4.2.4)

363 **6.3   Infrastructure**

364 The organization shall determine, provide and maintain the infrastructure needed to achieve conformity
365 to product requirements. Infrastructure includes, as applicable

366 a)   buildings, workspace and associated utilities,

367 b)   process equipment (both hardware and software), and

368 c)   supporting services (such as transport or communication).

Author's Notes

Change—Lines 363–368 are new in the 2000 version. Infrastructure was implied in the 1994 version. However, the 2000 version now requires infrastructure to be specifically addressed. Auditors will look for a process used to determine infrastructure requirements, perhaps in management review, and also, look for a follow-up to achieve infrastructure needs.

Compare with 4.1.2.2 Resources (1994):
"The supplier shall identify resource requirements and provide adequate resources, including the assignment of trained personnel (see 4.18), for management, performance of work, and verification activities, including internal quality audits."

Compare with 4.9 Process Control (1994):
"The supplier shall identify and plan the production, installation, and servicing processes which directly affect quality and shall ensure that these processes are carried out under controlled conditions. Controlled conditions shall include the following:
- ❑   Use of suitable production, installation, and servicing equipment and a suitable working environment;
- ❑   The approval of processes and equipment, as appropriate;
- ❑   Suitable maintenance of equipment to ensure continuing process capability."

Checklist

A.   Have we determined, provided, and maintained the infrastructure needed to achieve conformity to product requirements?

B.   Does infrastructure include, as applicable:
- ❑   Buildings, workspace, and associated utilities?
- ❑   Process equipment (both hardware and software)?
- ❑   Supporting services (such as transport or communication)?

---

369 **6.4   Work environment**

370 The organization shall determine and manage the work environment needed to achieve conformity to
371 product requirements.

Author's Notes

Clarification—The 1994 version required a "suitable working environment" in clause 4.9b. This new clause, 6.4 Work environment, makes it clear that achieving "conformity to product requirements" requires more than just comfort and housekeeping. It often involves physical factors, such as air purity, humidity, and temperature that may adversely affect processes. Organizations may have many varied processes for dealing with work environment. Some of those processes may include "5S," safety audits, housekeeping audits, ergonomics, ventilation controls, and establishing minimum lighting requirements.

Checklist

A.   Do we identify and manage the work environment needed to achieve conformity to product requirements?

---

372 # 7 Product realization

373 ## 7.1 Planning of product realization

374 The ~~supplier~~ organization shall ~~define~~ plan and ~~document~~ develop ~~how~~ the ~~requirements~~ processes
375 needed for ~~quality will be met~~ product realization. ~~Quality~~ Planning of product realization shall be consis-
376 tent with ~~all other~~ the requirements of ~~a supplier's~~ the other processes of the quality management system
377 ~~(see 4.1) and shall be documented in a format to suit the supplier's method of operation.~~

378 In planning product realization, the ~~supplier~~ organization shall ~~give consideration to~~ determine the follow-
379 ing ~~activities, as appropriate, in meeting the specified requirements for products, projects, or contracts:~~[1]

380 a) ~~the preparation of quality plans;~~ quality objectives and requirements for the product;

381 b) the ~~identification and acquisition~~ need to establish ~~of any controls,~~ processes, ~~equipment (including~~
382 ~~inspection and test equipment), fixtures,~~ documents, and provide resources, ~~and skills that may be~~
383 ~~needed to achieve the required quality~~ specific to the product;

384 c) ~~ensuring the compatibility of the design, the production process, installation, servicing, inspection, and~~
385 ~~test procedures, and the applicable documentation; d) the updating, as necessary, of quality control,~~
386 ~~inspection, and testing techniques, including the development of new instrumentation; e) the identifi-~~
387 ~~cation of any measurement requirement involving capability that exceeds the known state of the art,~~
388 ~~in sufficient time for the needed capability to be developed; f) the identification of suitable verification~~
389 ~~at appropriate stages in the realization of product;~~ required verification, validation, monitoring, inspec-
390 tion and test activities specific to the product and the criteria for product acceptance;

391 d) ~~h) the identification and preparation of quality records (see 4.16).~~ records needed to provide evidence
392 that the realization processes and resulting product meet requirements (see 4.2.4).

393 ~~g) the clarification of standards of acceptability for all features and requirements, including those which~~
394 ~~contain a subjective element;~~

395 ~~Quality~~ The output of this planning ~~shall be consistent with all other requirements of a supplier's quality~~
396 ~~system and~~ shall be ~~documented~~ in a ~~format~~ form ~~to suit~~ suitable for the ~~supplier's~~ organization's method
397 of operations.[2]

398 ~~NOTE 8   The quality plans referred to (see 4.2.3a) may be in the form of a reference to the appropriate~~
399 ~~documented procedures that form an integral part of the supplier's quality system.~~

400 NOTE 1   A document specifying the processes of the quality management system (including the
401 product realization processes) and the resources to be applied to a specific product, project or contract,
402 can be referred to as a quality plan.

403 NOTE 2   The organization may also apply the requirements given in 7.3 to the development of product
404 realization processes.

---

1.   Lines 375–380 were previously 4.2.3, paragraph 1 (1994). Line 381 (strikethrough) is addressed in 401–403.
2.   Lines 396–398 were previously 4.2.3, paragraph 1, sentence 2 (1994).

Author's Notes

Clarification—Lines 395–404, although there may not currently exist documents titled "Quality Plans," consider creating them (where it adds value) and developing a reference of the appropriate documentation, resources, and sequence of activities that are relevant to particular products, projects or contracts.

Should you elect *not* to have specific documents similar to or including quality plans, then you might consider developing a rationale statement indicating the justification for your decision and, as appropriate, identifying those documents that do serve as an output of the planning of product realization process.

Typically, control plans are used in lieu of quality plans, particularly in specific business sectors, such as automotive.

It is important to note that items a through d are issues (not necessarily requirements) that the organization shall, as appropriate, determine. An auditor will first determine what is being done with respect to planning of product realization, then evaluate the suitability and effectiveness of that planning activity.

Change—Item a, line 380, the requirement determining "quality objectives and requirements for the product" is new. The 1994 version assumed the customer would supply product quality requirements.

Item b now requires establishing processes and providing resources.

Lines 388–390, verification appeared in the 1994 version and is therefore not a change; however, validation is a change because it goes beyond verification. Validation may require prove-out testing, prototype testing, customer purchase part approval, and so on.

Lines 395–397, typical examples of "outputs" include control plans, quality plans, feasibility commitments, travelers, work orders, and so on.

Checklist

A. Do we plan and develop the processes needed for product realization?
B. Is the planning of product realization consistent with the requirements of the other processes of the quality management system? (see 4.1)
C. In planning product realization, have we determined the following, as appropriate:
   ❑ Quality objectives and requirements for the product?
   ❑ The need to establish processes, documents, and provide resources specific to the product?
   ❑ Required verification, validation, monitoring, inspection, and test activities specific to the product and the criteria for product acceptance?
   ❑ Records needed to provide evidence that the realization processes and resulting product meet requirements? (see 4.2.4)
D. Is the output of this planning in a form suitable for our method of operation?

405 ## 7.2   Customer-related processes

406 ## ~~4.3   Contract review~~

407 ### ~~4.3.1   General~~

408 ~~The supplier shall establish and maintain documented procedures for contract review and for the coordi-~~
409 ~~nation of these activities.~~

410 ### 7.2.1   Determination of requirements related to the product

411 The organization shall determine

412 a)   requirements specified by the customer, including the requirements for delivery and post-delivery
413   activities,

414 b)   requirements not stated by the customer but necessary for specified or intended use, where known,

415 c)   statutory and regulatory requirements related to the product, and

416 d)   any additional requirements determined by the organization.

Author's Notes

Relaxation—Lines 408 and 409, the requirement for a "documented procedure for contract review," is now deleted.

Change—Item a, the intent remains the same as in the 1994 version. However, specifically "including the requirements for delivery and post delivery activities" is new and will require these activities to be included "up front" in the requirements along with other specifications.

Item b is a new addition that highlights the difference between "requirements specified by the customer" and "customer requirements." The latter "customer requirements" includes both stated and unstated requirements. The organization must now anticipate intended use and, perhaps, customer needs, determine them and take them into consideration.

Clarification—Item c, line 415, statutory and regulatory requirements are specifically noted. Since they are often not provided by the customer they are easily overlooked and may have a high potential impact upon the quality management system and upon the deliverables to the customer.

Change—Item d, line 416, the organization may have specific requirements, such as reliability, life cycle, safety, and so on, that may go beyond the minimum customer, statutory, and regulatory requirements.

Checklist

A.   Have we determined:
- ❑   Requirements specified by the customer, including the requirements for delivery and post-delivery activities?
- ❑   Requirements not stated by the customer but necessary for specified or intended use, where known?
- ❑   Statutory and regulatory requirements related to the product?
- ❑   Any additional requirements?

417 **7.2.2** ~~**4.3.2**~~   **Review of requirements related to the product**

418 ~~Before~~ The organization shall review the requirements related to the product. This review shall be con-
419 ducted prior to the organization's commitment to supply a product to the customer (e.g. submission of a
420 tenders, ~~or at the~~ acceptance of a contracts or orders, acceptance of changes to contracts or orders)
421 ~~(statement of requirement), the tender, contract, or order shall be reviewed by the supplier to~~ and shall
422 ensure that~~:~~

423 a) ~~the~~ product requirements are ~~adequately~~ defined ~~and documented~~,

424 b) ~~any differences between the~~ contract or ~~accepted~~ order requirements ~~and those in the tender~~ differing
425   from those previously expressed are resolved, and

426 c) the ~~supplier~~ organization has the ~~capability~~ ability to meet ~~the contract or accepted order~~ the defined
427   requirements.

428 **4.3.4**   **Records**

429 Records of the results of the ~~contract~~ reviews and actions arising from the review shall be maintained (see
430 ~~4.16~~ 4.2.4).

431 Where the customer provides no ~~written~~ documented statement of requirement~~, is available for an order~~
432 ~~received by verbal means~~ the ~~supplier~~ customer requirements shall ~~ensure that the order requirements~~
433 ~~are agreed~~ be confirmed by the organization before ~~their~~ acceptance.[1]

434 **4.3.3**   **Amendment to contract**

435 ~~The supplier shall identify how an amendment to a contract is made and correctly transferred to the~~
436 ~~functions concerned within the supplier's organization.~~ Where product requirements are changed, the
437 organization shall ensure that relevant documents are amended and that relevant personnel are made
438 aware of the changed requirements.

439 NOTE   In some situations, such as internet sales, a formal review is impractical for each order. Instead
440 the review can cover relevant product information, such as catalogues or advertising material.

---

1.   Lines 432–434 were previously included in 4.3.2 a (1994)

Author's Notes

Clarification—The term *ability* in item c implies having the facilities, staff, inventory, expertise, and so on to satisfy contract or order requirements. Review of requirements is used here in a sense that may go beyond the review of requirements found under Contract Review in the 1994 version. Here the activity includes understanding the customer requirements to the extent that they are adequately defined and agreed to. Determining customer requirements and verifying the organization's capability to meet these requirements is an essential element of the quality management system. Lines 417–427 now address agreement, resolution, and ability to meet requirements of any order including verbal orders.

Lines 429 and 430, records must be maintained to demonstrate the communication of contract amendments to affected areas, such as production control, design functions, customer service, purchasing, and so on.

Lines 431–433 address confirmation of orders with no statement of requirements including verbal orders. Also, lines 429–433 clarify that absence of a "documented statement of requirements," such as verbal orders and agreements need to be confirmed with all affected parties prior to acceptance.

Lines 435–440 will require either a process addressing contract amendment or that the existing procedure is updated to provide for the transfer of order changes to all concerned functions. To assess this clause, search for the occurrence of amendments in the order(s) (purchase order[s]) or contract(s), then determine whether these changes were communicated back to the affected "relevant personnel" or functional groups. Typically, amendments to contract are reviewed and communicated via change notices.

Auditors will look for evidence or records of actual communication activity to compare against established internal procedures, processes or instructions. Auditors should also look for:

- ❑ Clear definition of contract scope
- ❑ Adequate determination and documentation of requirements
- ❑ Identification and resolution of any variation from the original proposal(s) and or contract
- ❑ Effective handling of contract amendments

Checklist

A. Do we review the requirements related to the product?
B. Is the review conducted prior to our commitment to supply a product to the customer (for example, submission of tenders, acceptance of contracts or orders, acceptance of changes to contracts or orders)?
C. Does the review ensure that:
- ❑ Product requirements are defined?
- ❑ Contract or order requirements differing from those previously expressed are resolved?
- ❑ We have the ability to meet the defined requirements?
D. Are records of the results of the review and actions arising from the review maintained? (see 4.2.4)
E. Where the customer provides no documented statement of requirement, have we confirmed the customer requirements before acceptance?
F. Where product requirements are changed, have we ensured that relevant documents are amended?
G. Have we ensured that relevant personnel are made aware of the changed requirements?

441 **7.2.3**   **Customer communication**

442 ~~NOTE 9~~   ~~Channels for communication and interfaces with the customer's organization in these contract~~
443 ~~matters should be established.~~[1] The organization shall determine and implement effective arrangements
444 for communicating with customers in relation to

445 a)   product information,

446 b)   enquiries, contracts or order handling, including amendments, and

447 c)   customer feedback, including customer complaints.

Author's Notes

Change—Although Annex B (in the back of the standard) links this clause with 4.3.2 Review in *ISO 9001:1994,* the customer communication addressed here in the 2000 version goes beyond that in the 1994 version.

Line 445, item a, the organization must communicate with customers about "product information." This could also include product promotional and/or marketing information.

Line 446, item b, previously in the 1994 version, communication included "contract matters." Item b, lines 440 and 441, is much broader in scope.

Line 447, item c, customer complaints were previously addressed in the 1994 version. However, "customer feedback" broadened this to include *all* customer feedback in the 2000 version.

Checklist

A.   Do we determine and implement effective arrangements for communicating with customers in relation to:
- ❑   Product information?
- ❑   Enquiries, contracts, or order handling, including amendments?
- ❑   Customer feedback, including customer complaints?

---

448 **7.3** ~~4.4~~   **Design ~~control~~ and development**

449 **~~4.4.1~~**   **~~General~~**

450 ~~The supplier shall establish and maintain documented procedures to control and verify the design of the~~
451 ~~product in order to ensure that the specified requirements are met.~~

452 **7.3.1** ~~4.4.2~~   **Design and development planning**

453 The ~~supplier~~ organization shall ~~prepare plans for each~~ plan and control the design and development of
454 product ~~activity. The plans shall describe or reference these activities, and define responsibility for their~~
455 ~~implementation. The design and development activities shall be assigned to qualified personnel equipped~~
456 ~~with adequate resources.~~

457 During the design and development planning, the organization shall determine

458 a)   the design and development stages,

459 b)   the review, verification and validation that are appropriate to each design and development stage, and

460 c)   the responsibilities and authorities for design and development.

461 **~~4.4.3~~**   **~~Organizational and technical interfaces~~**

462 The organization shall manage the ~~Organizational and technical~~ interfaces between different groups ~~which~~
463 ~~input into the~~ involved in design ~~process~~ and development ~~shall be defined and the necessary information~~

---

1.   Lines 443, 444 were previously under 4.3.4 (1994).

464 ~~documented, transmitted, and regularly reviewed~~ to ensure effective communication and clear assignment
465 of responsibility.

466 ~~The plans~~ Planning output shall be updated, as appropriate, as the design and development ~~evolves~~
467 progresses.[1]

Author's Notes

When design milestones are not met, look for:
- ❑ A documented shift in priorities dictated by the customer
- ❑ Qualifications of the team members
- ❑ Poor planning on the part of project planners

Change—Design and development planning now specifically includes the clear determination of:
- ❑ Design and development stages
- ❑ Review, verification, and validation, as appropriate, at each stage
- ❑ Responsibilities and authorities

Activity assignment is part of planning. Planning output must be updated after significant changes.

Clarification—The interface must be managed. This subclause requires an identification of and clear communication between the various contributors to the design process, such as:
- ❑ Research and development
- ❑ Marketing
- ❑ Purchasing
- ❑ Quality assurance
- ❑ Engineering
- ❑ Materials
- ❑ Production

Checklist

A. Do we plan and control the design and development of product?
B. During the design and development planning, do we determine:
- ❑ The design and development stages?
- ❑ The review, verification, and validation that is appropriate to each design and development stage?
- ❑ The responsibilities and authorities for design and development?
C. Are interfaces between different groups involved in design and development managed to ensure effective communication and clear assignment of responsibility?
D. Is planning output updated, as appropriate, as the design and development progresses?

---

1. Lines 467, 468 were previously 4.4.2, sentence 4 (1994).

468 **7.3.2 4.4.4**   **Design and development inputs**

469 ~~Design~~-Inputs ~~requirements~~ relating to ~~the~~ product~~, including applicable statutory and regulatory~~ require-
470 ~~ments,~~ shall be ~~identified,~~ determined and records maintained (see 4.2.4) ~~documented,~~. These inputs
471 shall include

472 a)   functional and performance requirements,

473 b)   applicable statutory and regulatory requirements,

474 c)   where applicable, information derived from previous similar designs, and

475 d)   other requirements essential for design and development.

476 These inputs shall be ~~and their selection~~ reviewed ~~by the supplier~~ for adequacy. ~~Incomplete, ambiguous,~~
477 ~~or conflicting~~ Requirements shall be complete, unambiguous and not in conflict with each other ~~resolved~~
478 ~~with those responsible for imposing these requirements~~.

479 ~~Design input shall take into consideration the results of any contract-review activities.~~

Author's Notes

Clarification—A master design document, such as a project plan with or without design review checklists, could serve to satisfy the requirements of items a–d. Such a document would:

- ❏   Reflect agreement of the customer and the organization of functional and performance requirements
- ❏   Follow the design throughout the process
- ❏   Have a change or review process

Statutory and regulatory requirements are specifically noted since they are often not provided by the customer, are easily overlooked, and may have a high potential impact upon the quality management system.

The organization is obligated to ensure that design input requirements and the applicable statutory and regulatory requirements are identified during the design input phase, rather than being uncovered later in the design process.

A link is made between the determination of customer requirements (7.2.1 and 7.2.2) and the determination of the design requirements (design input). See also 5.2 Customer focus.

Change—Lines 469–471, records must now be maintained for items a through d, lines 472–475.

Checklist

A.   Are inputs relating to product requirements determined and records maintained? (see 4.2.4)
B.   Do inputs and records include
     ❏   Functional and performance requirements?
     ❏   Applicable statutory and regulatory requirements?
     ❏   Where applicable, information derived from previous similar designs?
     ❏   Any other requirements essential for design and development?
C.   Are the inputs reviewed for adequacy?
D.   Are requirements complete, unambiguous, and not in conflict with each other?

7.3.3 ~~4.4.5~~ Design and development outputs

481 ~~Design~~ The outputs of design and development shall be ~~documented~~ provided in a form that enables
482 verification ~~and expressed in terms that can be verified~~ against the design and development input and
483 shall be approved prior to release ~~requirements and validated (see 4.4.8)~~.

484 Design and development outputs shall~~:~~

485 a) meet the ~~design~~ input requirements for design and development,

486 b) provide appropriate information for purchasing, production and for service provision,

487 c) ~~b)~~ contain or ~~make~~ reference ~~to~~ product acceptance criteria, and

488 d) ~~c) identify those~~ specify the characteristics of the ~~design~~ product that are ~~crucial~~ essential ~~to the~~ for
489   its safe and proper ~~functioning~~ use ~~of the product (e.g., operating, storage, handling, maintenance,~~
490   ~~and disposal requirements)~~.

491 ~~Design-output documents shall be reviewed before release.~~[1]

Author's Notes

Clarification—Examples of design and development outputs are drawings, instructions, software, functional test procedures, in-process test specifications, test equipment, and so on. Design and development output should reflect design-input requirements.

It is more appropriate to express the desired output in terms that can be verified and validated. Not all design outputs need be expressed in terms of calculations nor analyses.

Design output is still required to meet the input criteria and identify characteristics crucial to the safe and proper functioning of the product. There is also a requirement that "design and development output" be approved before release. The release could be at the completion of appropriate design stages or it could be the final release.

Change—Line 486, item b, although probably a deliverable of the initial design review, providing purchasing, production, and service information is a specified requirement and no longer left to chance.

Checklist

A. Are the outputs of the design and development provided in a form that enables verification against the design and development inputs?

B. Are the outputs of the design and development approved prior to release?

C. Do the design and development outputs:
   ❑ Meet the input requirements for design and development?
   ❑ Provide appropriate information for purchasing, production, and for service provision?
   ❑ Contain or reference product acceptance criteria?
   ❑ Specify the characteristics of the product that are essential for its safe and proper use?

---

1. Line 492 (strikethrough) is addressed in the 2000 version in line 484.

492 **7.3.4** 4.4.6   Design and development review

493 At ~~appropriate~~ suitable stages ~~of design,~~ ~~formal documented~~ systematic reviews of ~~the~~ design and devel-
494 opment ~~results~~ shall be ~~planned and conducted~~ performed in accordance with planned arrangements (see
495 7.3.1)

496 a)   to evaluate the ability of the results of design and development to meet requirements, and

497 b)   to identify any problems and propose necessary actions.

498 Participants ~~at each design~~ in such reviews shall include representatives of ~~all~~ functions concerned with
499 the design and development stage(s) being reviewed, ~~as well as other specialist personnel, as required~~.
500 Records of the results of the ~~such~~ reviews and any necessary actions shall be maintained (see ~~4.16~~
501 4.2.4).

Author's Notes

Clarification—Design validation and design verification are specific types of design review.

Design reviews that include representatives of functions concerned shall be held and documented or recorded in the form of meeting agenda, meeting minutes, list of attendees, and so on. The stages at which the review are performed need to be clearly defined.

Design review activity may result in modification of some design planning activities.

Depending on the nature of the organization (size, industry sector, and so on), it is important that all appropriate functions affected by the design stage under review be represented during the review. This provides the broad view originally captured by the concept of independent reviewers and counterbalances the danger of designers approving their own work. More important, however, is the communication, cooperation, and exchange of expertise among functional groups to contribute to the overall design process.

Lines 496 and 497 are just clarifying the intent and practice that is typical of a design review.

Checklist

A.   At suitable stages, are systematic reviews of design and development performed in accordance with planned arrangements (see 7.3.1) to:
- ❑   Evaluate the ability of the results of design and development to meet requirements?
- ❑   Identify any problems and propose necessary actions?

B.   Do participants in such reviews include representatives of functions concerned with the design and development stage(s) being reviewed?

C.   Are records of the results of the reviews and any necessary actions maintained? (see 4.2.4)

502 **7.3.5** ~~4.4.7~~ **Design and development verification**

503 ~~At appropriate stages of design, design~~ Verification shall be performed in accordance with planned
504 arrangements (see 7.3.1) to ensure that the design-~~stage~~ and development outputs ~~meets~~ have met the
505 design and development ~~stage~~ input requirements. ~~The design-verification measures~~ Records of the
506 results of the verification and any necessary actions shall be ~~recorded~~ maintained (see ~~4.16~~ 4.2.4).

507 ~~NOTE 10   In addition to conducting design reviews (see 4.4.6), design verification may include activities,~~
508 ~~such as~~

509 ~~— performing alternative calculations,~~

510 ~~— comparing the new design with a similar proven design, if available,~~

511 ~~— undertaking tests and demonstrations, and~~

512 ~~— reviewing the design-stage documents before release.~~

Author's Notes

NOTE 10 identifying typical means of design verification in the 1994 version has been deleted. However, these same methods may continue to be used for design verification.

Clarification—The crossed out words in lines 505 and 506 appear to represent a change. Instead of recording "design verification measures," the 2000 version requires maintaining "records of the results of the verification and any necessary actions." While "verification measures" and "verification results" are different, the overall intent of the clause remains unchanged.

Checklist

A. Is verification performed in accordance with planned arrangements (see 7.3.1) to ensure that the design and development outputs have met the design and development input requirements?
B. Are records of the results of the verification and any necessary actions maintained? (see 4.2.4)

513 **7.3.6 4.4.8** **Design and development validation**

514 Design and development validation shall be performed in accordance with planned arrangements (see
515 7.3.1) to ensure that the resulting product ~~conforms to defined user needs and/or~~ is capable of meeting
516 the requirements for the specified application or intended use, where known. Wherever practicable,
517 validation shall be completed prior to the delivery or implementation of the product. Records of the results
518 of validation and any necessary actions shall be maintained (see 4.2.4).

519 ~~NOTES~~

520 ~~11 Design validation follows successful design verification (see 4.4.7).~~

521 ~~12 Validation is normally performed under defined operating conditions.~~

522 ~~13 Validation is normally performed on the final product, but may be necessary in earlier stages prior to~~
523 ~~product completion.~~

524 ~~14 Multiple validations may be performed if there are different intended uses.~~

Author's Notes

Design validation ties back to customer requirements and ensures that requirements are met. This involves customer input on the design, the end use application, and/or environmental conditions.

Typically, validation requirements are agreed on by both the customer and the organization.

Examples of design validation may involve product performance testing at maximum end use conditions prior to completing the design. Examples of validation tests may include impact test, accelerated corrosion tests, temperature cycling, over/under voltage performance tests, and so on. In some industries a design verification plan and report (DVP&R) along with the production part approval process (PPAP) satisfies both validation and verification requirements.

For service industries, process validation may be linked with customer acceptance, expected results, and so on.

The NOTES formerly highlighted the difference between verification (does design stage output meet design stage input requirements?) and validation (does the product satisfy user needs?). Consequently, it is possible to have a design that is successful in every verification phase, but fails to satisfy some or all user needs.

Change—Previous versions of ISO 9001 do not specifically require validation "*prior* to delivery or implementation of the product."

Checklist

A. Is design and development validation performed in accordance with planned arrangements (see 7.3.1) to ensure that the resulting product is capable of meeting the requirements for the specified application or intended use, where known?
B. Wherever practicable, is validation completed prior to the delivery or implementation of the product?
C. Are records of the results of validation and any necessary actions maintained? (see 4.2.4)

525 **7.3.7 4.4.9   Control of design and development changes**

526 All Design and development changes and modifications shall be identified, documented, reviewed, and
527 records maintained. The changes shall be reviewed, verified and validated, as appropriate, and approved
528 by authorized personnel before their implementation. The review of design and development changes
529 shall include evaluation of the effect of the changes on constituent parts and product already delivered.

530 Records of the results of the review of changes and any necessary actions shall be maintained (see
531 4.2.4).

Author's Notes

A formal design and development change process, procedure or work instruction is needed to ensure that design changes are controlled and communicated properly. Typically, an engineering change notice (ECN) is used to communicate and review changes. Where it is not obvious, the point of delivery and/or implementation must be defined.

Change—Note that the phrase "before implementation," line 528, indicates changes and modifications must be identified, reviewed, approved, verified, and validated *before* those changes are actually implemented. Define at what point design changes are considered implemented.

Change—The statement in line 527, "changes shall be … verified and validated," indicates that any changes after the verification and/or validation stages require reverification and/or revalidation "as appropriate."

Checklist

A. Are design and development changes identified and records maintained?
B. Are changes reviewed, verified, and validated, as appropriate, and approved before implementation?
C. Does the review of design and development changes include evaluation of the effect of the changes on constituent parts and product already delivered?
D. Are records of the results of the review of changes and any necessary actions maintained? (see 4.2.4)

532 **7.4** 4.6   **Purchasing**

533 **7.4.1** 4.6.1   ~~General~~ Purchasing process

534 The ~~supplier~~ organization shall ~~establish and maintain documented procedures to~~ ensure that purchased
535 product ~~(see 3.1)~~ conforms to specified purchase requirements. ~~b) define~~ The type and extent of control
536 ~~exercised~~ applied ~~by the supplier over subcontractors.~~ to the supplier and the purchased product shall be
537 dependent upon the ~~type of product, the impact of subcontracted product on the quality of final product,~~
538 ~~and, where applicable, on the quality audit reports and/or quality records of the previously demonstrated~~
539 ~~capability and performance of subcontractors;~~ effect of the purchased product on subsequent product
540 realization or the final product.[1]

541 **4.6.2**   **Evaluation of subcontractors**

542 The ~~supplier~~ organization shall~~:~~

543 a)   evaluate and select ~~subcontractors~~ suppliers based on ~~the basis of~~ their ability to ~~meet subcontract~~
544   supply product in accordance with the organization's requirements. ~~including the quality system and~~
545   ~~any specific quality-assurance requirements;~~

546 ~~c)   establish and maintain quality records of acceptable subcontractors (see 4.16).~~

547 Criteria for selection, evaluation and re-evaluation shall be established. Records of the results of evalua-
548 tions and any necessary actions arising from the evaluation shall be maintained (see 4.2.4).

Author's Notes

Clarification—Criteria for choosing a supplier might be previous performance, ISO assessment, supplier assessment, receiving and inspection records, testing of samples, written surveys, and so on.

It is still possible to have dock-to-stock or ship-to-stock suppliers if you have a system for doing so and traceability
of materials. Some raw materials can only be inspected at the operators' point of use. An example of this might be
rolls of coated sheet metal.

Records here could be as simple as an approved supplier list or could be more detailed to include records for each
supplier's ongoing compliance with specifications, costs, delivery dates, ongoing tests, and evaluations.

The organization defines the type and extent of control it exercises over suppliers. The organization shall consider
"the effect of purchased product on the subsequent product or processes in determining the extent of controls."
Auditors will seek to verify that these items were actually considered when defining the extent of controls and that
records of acceptable subcontractors are established and maintained.

Checklist

A.   Do we ensure that purchased product conforms to specified purchase requirements?
B.   Is the type and extent of control applied to the supplier and the purchased product dependent upon the ef-
     fect of the purchased product on subsequent product realization or the final product?
C.   Have we evaluated and selected suppliers based on their ability to supply product in accordance with our
     requirements?
D.   Are the criteria for selection, evaluation, and re-evaluation established?
E.   Are records of the results of evaluations, and any necessary actions arising from the evaluation main-
     tained? (see 4.2.4)

---

1.   Lines 535–540 were previously 4.6.2.b (1994).

549 **7.4.2** ~~4.6.3~~ **Purchasing ~~data~~ information**

550 Purchasing ~~documents~~ information shall ~~contain data clearly describing~~ describe the product to be pur-
551 chased ~~ordered~~, including where ~~applicable~~ appropriate

552 a) ~~the type, class, grade, or other precise identification; b) the title or other positive identification, and~~
553 ~~applicable issues of specifications, drawings, process requirements, inspection instructions, and other~~
554 ~~relevant technical data, including~~ requirements for approval or ~~qualification~~ of product, procedures,
555 ~~process equipment,~~ processes and equipment ~~and personnel,~~

556 b) requirements for qualification of personnel, and ⟶ △ *where appropriate*

557 c) ~~the title, number, and issue of the~~ quality management system ~~standard to be applied~~ requirements.

558 The ~~supplier~~ organization shall ~~review and approve purchasing documents for~~ ensure the adequacy of
559 the specified purchase requirements prior to ~~release~~ their communication to the supplier.

Author's Notes

This purchasing information section typically applies to all of the following: material going directly into the product, tools, and equipment used in the production of the product, and evaluation of subcontracted services, such as calibration, trucking, maintenance, and surveillance. Be sure that specifications are accurately communicated in a timely manner.

Change—Generally, this clause is unchanged in intent from the 1994 version, except item b, line 556, represents a change in requiring specific "requirements for qualification of personnel." This may not be practical depending on the complexity and criticality of purchased product. A rationale statement as to why this is not a value add or why it is not appropriate should be in place. Item b should not be mentioned in the scope statement under permissible exclusions since line 551 specifically states "… including *where appropriate*."

Checklist

A. Does our purchasing information describe the product to be purchased, including, where appropriate:
   ❑ Requirements for approval of:
   • Product?
   • Procedures?
   • Processes?
   • Equipment?
   ❑ Requirements for qualification of personnel?
   ❑ Quality management system requirements?
B. Do we ensure the adequacy of specified purchase requirements prior to their communication to the supplier?

45

560 **7.4.3** **4.6.4**   **Verification of purchased product**

561 **4.10.2**   ~~Receiving inspection and testing~~

562 **4.10.2.1**   ~~The supplier shall ensure that incoming product is not used or processed (except in the~~
563 ~~circumstances described in 4.10.2.3) until it has been inspected or otherwise verified as conforming to~~
564 ~~specified requirements. Verification of the specified requirements shall be in accordance with the quality~~
565 ~~plan and/or documented procedures.~~

566 **4.10.2.2**   ~~In determining the amount and nature of receiving inspection, consideration shall be given~~
567 ~~to the amount of control exercised at the subcontractor's premises and the recorded evidence of confor-~~
568 ~~mance provided.~~

569 **4.10.2.3**   ~~Where incoming product is released for urgent production purposes~~ prior to ~~verification, it~~
570 ~~shall be positively identified and recorded (see 4.16) in order to permit immediate recall and replacement~~
571 ~~in the event of nonconformity to specified requirements.~~

572 The organization shall establish and implement the inspection or other activities necessary for ensuring
573 that purchased product meets specified purchase requirements.

574 **4.6.4.1**   ~~Supplier verification at subcontractor's premises~~

575 Where the ~~supplier~~ organization or its customer ~~proposes~~ intends to ~~verify purchased product~~ perform
576 verification at the ~~subcontractor's~~ supplier's premises, the ~~supplier~~ organization shall ~~specify~~ state the
577 intended verification arrangements and ~~the~~ method of product release in the purchasing ~~documents~~
578 information.

579 **4.6.4.2**   ~~Customer verification of subcontracted product~~

580 ~~Where specified in the contract, the supplier's customer or the customer's representative shall be afforded~~
581 ~~the right to verify at the subcontractor's premises and the supplier's premises that subcontracted product~~
582 ~~conforms to specified requirements. Such verification shall not be used by the supplier as evidence of~~
583 ~~effective control of quality by the subcontractor.~~

584 ~~Verification by the customer shall not absolve the supplier of the responsibility to provide acceptable~~
585 ~~product, nor shall~~ it ~~preclude subsequent rejection by the customer.~~

Author's Notes

Clarification—Although far less prescriptive, as evidenced by the amount of strikethrough text, the intent and
degree purchased product is to be verified remains unchanged. Lines 572 and 573 do not preclude the use of dock-
to-stock or ship-to-stock suppliers. Incoming inspection and test may be waived if you have a documented means
of evaluating and qualifying those suppliers to ensure requirements are met. A dock-to-stock process would fall
under the phrase "other activities."

Depending on the product or service that you provide, visits to suppliers premises may not be practical. Lines 575–
578 have the same intent as 4.6.4.1 from the 1994 version. As auditors, we should verify that these arrangements
are defined and agreed to by all concerned parties if onsite verification is to be performed by the organization.

Checklist

A. Have we established and implemented the inspection or other activities necessary for ensuring that pur-
    chased product meets specified purchase requirements?
B. Where we or our customer intend to perform verification at the supplier's premises, have we stated the in-
    tended verification arrangements and method of product release in the purchasing information?

7.5   Production and service provision

7.5.1 ~~4.9~~   ~~Process~~ Control of production and service provision

The ~~supplier~~ organization shall ~~identify and~~ plan ~~the~~ and carry out production~~, installation,~~ and service provision ~~servicing processes which directly affect quality and shall ensure that these processes are carried out~~ under controlled conditions. Controlled conditions shall include~~, the following~~ as applicable:

a) ~~documented procedures defining the manner of production, installation, and servicing, where the absence of such procedures could adversely affect quality;~~ the availability of information that describes the characteristics of the product,

b) ~~f) criteria for workmanship, which shall be stipulated in the clearest practical manner (e.g., written standards, representative samples, or illustrations);~~ the availability of work instructions, as necessary,

c) ~~b)~~ the use of suitable ~~production, installation, and servicing~~ equipment, ~~and a suitable working environment; c) compliance with reference standards/codes, quality plans, and/or documented procedures;~~

d) the availability and use of monitoring and measuring devices, ~~and control of suitable process parameters and product characteristics;~~

e) ~~the approval of processes and equipment, as appropriate;~~ the implementation of monitoring and measurement, and

f) the implementation of release, delivery and post-delivery activities.

g) ~~suitable maintenance of equipment to ensure continuing process capability.~~

4.19   Servicing

~~Where servicing is a specified requirement, the supplier shall establish and maintain documented procedures for performing, verifying, and reporting that the servicing meets the specified requirements.~~

Author's Notes

Lines 586–600. Using suitable (capable) and controlled processes to produce, install, and service the product is an important form of prevention. Process capability studies, with their incorporated statistical analyses, are often used to determine suitability and control of the equipment and to determine impact of environmental conditions. Monitoring and control of these processes are often performed by the use of statistical process control.

"Service provision" in lines 588 and 589 replaces the former term "servicing." Service provision is required and is sufficiently broad in scope to include internal and external service activities. Determine if service is an integral part of the product or deliverables to the customer. If yes, then evaluate servicing equipment to determine which requires control. Some companies do not provide servicing. Recognizing this, the standard allows the organization to include service provision as a permissible exclusion under clause 1.2.

Clarification—The deletion of line 604 shows maintenance as deleted. However, it is picked up elsewhere only by implication in line 596, "the use of suitable equipment," in clause 7.5.1c. Equipment that is not maintained typically is not suitable. Light maintenance of equipment may be performed routinely by the operator, such as lubricating and cleaning machines periodically.

Assessment of the maintenance program depends on what the organization defines maintenance to be and includes adequate records of maintenance activity. Maintenance tends to not relate well to the service category and may be difficult for an organization such as a small service business to embrace.

Clarification—Item b takes into account the workers' skill in determining the type of procedures or work instructions. You may also include samples, drawings, or pictures to supplement or convey work instructions.

Clarification—Items c, d, and e represent a clarification and no change of intent.

Change—Item f is a change and now requires delivery and post-delivery activities. To assess this, search for release, delivery, and post delivery (where appropriate) being included in the identified processes.

Clarification—Documented procedures are no longer mandated for servicing, line 591. However, if you already have them in place and they are adding value, you are under no obligation to delete them. Line 595 makes it clear that, where necessary, work instructions must be available.

Checklist

A. Do we plan and carry out production and service provision under controlled conditions? Controlled conditions include, as applicable, the:
- ☐ Availability of information that describes the characteristics of the product
- ☐ Availability of work instructions, as necessary
- ☐ Use of suitable equipment
- ☐ Availability and use of monitoring and measuring devices
- ☐ Implementation of monitoring and measurement
- ☐ Implementation of release, delivery, and post-delivery activities

608 **7.5.2 Validation of processes for production and service provision**

609 The organization shall validate any processes for production and service provision where the ~~results of~~
610 ~~processes cannot be fully~~ resulting output cannot be verified by subsequent ~~inspection and testing of the~~
611 ~~product and where, for example, processing~~ monitoring or measurement. This includes any processes
612 where deficiencies ~~may~~ become apparent only after the product is in use~~,~~ or the service has been deliv-
613 ered. ~~the processes shall be carried out by qualified operators and/or shall require continuous monitoring~~
614 ~~and control of process parameters to ensure that the specified requirements are met.~~

615 Validation shall demonstrate the ability of these processes to achieve planned results.

616 ~~The requirements for any qualification of process operations, including associated equipment and person-~~
617 ~~nel (see 4.18), shall be specified.~~ The organization shall establish arrangements for these processes
618 including, as applicable

619 a) defined criteria for review and approval of the processes,

620 b) approval of equipment and qualification of personnel,

621 c) use of specific methods and procedures,

622 d) ~~Records shall be maintained for qualified processes, equipment, and personnel, as appropriate (see~~
623   ~~4.16).~~ requirements for records (see 4.2.4), and

624 e) revalidation.

625 ~~NOTE 16   Such processes requiring prequalification of their process capability are frequently referred~~
626 ~~to as special processes.~~

Author's Notes

Change—Lines 609 and 610. Process validation, while advisable for any process, is required for those processes often referred to as special processes.

Such processes might include soldering, brazing, welding or the use of electrostatic discharge protection in dealing with ESD sensitive material. There is not a separate sub clause for special processes, this being incorporated into the main clause on control of production and service provision. The process control requirements for other products apply also to these products of special processes. The product categories of processed materials and software often fall into this area, where the results of processes cannot be fully verified by inspection and test.

Checklist

A. Do we validate any processes for production and service provision where the resulting output cannot be verified by subsequent monitoring or measurement?
B. Does this include any processes where deficiencies become apparent only after the product is in use or the service has been delivered?
C. Does validation demonstrate the ability of these processes to achieve planned results?
D. Have we established arrangements for these processes including, as applicable:
  ❑ Defined criteria for review and approval of the processes?
  ❑ Approval of equipment and qualification of personnel?
  ❑ Use of specific methods and procedures?
  ❑ Requirements for records? (see 4.2.4)
  ❑ Revalidation?

627 **7.5.3** **4.8** ~~Product~~ Identification and traceability

628 Where appropriate, the ~~supplier~~ organization shall ~~establish and maintain documented procedures for~~
629 ~~identifying~~ identify the product by suitable means ~~from receipt and during all stages of~~ throughout ~~produc-~~
630 ~~tion, delivery, and installation~~ product realization.

631 **4.12** **Inspection and test status**

632 ~~The inspection and test status of product shall be identified by suitable means, which indicate the confor-~~
633 ~~mance or nonconformance of product with regard to inspection and tests performed. The identification~~
634 ~~of inspection and test status shall be maintained, as defined in the quality plan and/or documented proce-~~
635 ~~dures, throughout production, installation, and servicing of the product to ensure that only product that has~~
636 ~~passed the required inspections and tests [or released under an authorized concession (see 4.13.2)] is~~
637 ~~dispatched, used, or installed.~~

638 The organization shall identify the product status with respect to monitoring and measurement require-
639 ments.

640 Where ~~and to the extent that~~ traceability is a ~~specified~~ requirement, the ~~supplier~~ organization shall estab-
641 ~~lish and maintain documented procedures for~~ control and record the unique identification of ~~individual~~ the
642 product ~~or batches. This identification shall be recorded~~ (see ~~4.16~~ 4.2.4).

643 NOTE   In some industry sectors, configuration management is a means by which identification and
644 traceability are maintained.

Author's Notes

Clarification—"Where appropriate" leaves a lot of latitude. The main thing is to decide if identification and traceability is a requirement, then decide how you will comply with that decision. Usually a date code is sufficient. Consider whether or not there is an industry norm or regulatory requirement for identification and traceability.

The organization has considerable latitude to decide an appropriate means of identification. Identification of incoming product falls within the scope of this activity.

Verify that inspection and test records are specifically mentioned in the records procedure (4.2.4).

These concepts are easily understood for all product categories. There is an important distinction between controlling quality and preventing defects emphasized through process control and the verification that specified require ments are met. Both of these activities are important and apply to all product categories.

Status should be very clear to indicate if a product has been:
- ❏ Inspected (or not)
- ❏ Accepted (or not)
- ❏ Put on hold
- ❏ Rejected and/or quarantined

With the number of words deleted, this appears to be a relaxation and, except for the deletion of the words in line 628 "documented procedures," the intent to have an appropriate degree of traceability of product remains unchanged.

Checklist

A.   Where appropriate, do we identify the product by suitable means throughout product realization?
B.   Do we identify the product status with respect to monitoring and measurement requirements?
C.   Where traceability is a requirement, do we control and record the unique identification of the product? (see 4.2.4)

645 **7.5.4** ~~4.7~~ ~~Control of~~ Customer ~~supplied product~~ **property**

646 The ~~supplier~~ organization shall ~~establish and maintain documented procedures for the control of verifica-~~
647 ~~tion, storage, and maintenance of~~ exercise care with customer ~~supplied product provided for incorporation~~
648 ~~into the supplies or for related activities~~ property while it is under the organization's control or being used
649 by the organization. The organization shall identify, verify, protect and safeguard customer property
650 provided for use or incorporation into the product. ~~Any such product~~ If any customer property ~~that~~ is lost,
651 damaged, ~~or is~~ otherwise found to be unsuitable for use, this shall be ~~recorded and~~ reported to the cus-
652 tomer ~~and records maintained~~ (see ~~4.16~~ 4.2.4).

653 ~~Verification by the supplier does not absolve the customer of the responsibility to provide acceptable~~
654 ~~product.~~

655 NOTE   Customer property can include intellectual property.

Author's Notes

Clarification—Customer property now replaces customer-supplied product. The new term clarifies that customer-supplied tooling, packaging, intellectual property, raw material, or other customer property all may be considered within the scope of customer property. Many companies handle customer property in the same manner and under the same procedures and work instructions as purchased product. If customer property requires unique handling or unique processes because it is customer property, then address that under this clause. Make sure, however, that you have a mechanism or means of communicating a nonconformity back to the customer that is acceptable to or prescribed by the customer.

Checklist

A.   Do we exercise care with customer property while it is under our control or while we are using it?
B.   Do we:
  ❑ Identify
  ❑ Verify
  ❑ Protect
  ❑ Safeguard
  customer property provided for use or incorporation into the product?
C.   Is any customer property that is lost, damaged, or otherwise found to be unsuitable for use reported to the customer? (see 4.2.4)
D.   Are records maintained for customer property that is lost, damaged, or otherwise found to be unsuitable for use? (see 4.2.4)

656 **7.5.5**   Preservation of product

657 **4.15**   ~~Handling, storage, packaging, preservation, and delivery~~

658 **4.15.1**   ~~General~~

659 ~~The supplier shall establish and maintain documented procedures for handling, storage, packaging,~~
660 ~~preservation, and delivery of product.~~

661 **4.15.2**   ~~Handling~~

662 ~~The supplier shall provide methods of handling product that prevent damage or deterioration.~~

663 **4.15.3**   ~~Storage~~

664 ~~The supplier shall use designated storage areas or stock rooms to prevent damage or deterioration of~~
665 ~~product, pending use or delivery. Appropriate methods for authorizing receipt to and dispatch from such~~
666 ~~areas shall be stipulated.~~

667 ~~In order to detect deterioration, the condition of product in stock shall be assessed at appropriate intervals.~~

668 **4.15.4**   ~~Packaging~~

669 ~~The supplier shall control packing, packaging, and marking processes (including materials used) to the~~
670 ~~extent necessary to ensure conformance to specified requirements.~~

671 **4.15.5**   ~~Preservation~~

672 ~~The supplier shall apply appropriate methods for preservation and segregation of product when the~~
673 ~~product is under the supplier's control.~~

674 **4.15.6**   ~~Delivery~~

675 ~~The supplier shall arrange for the protection of the quality of product after final inspection and test. Where~~
676 ~~contractually specified, this protection shall be extended to include delivery to destination.~~

677 The organization shall preserve the conformity of product during internal processing and delivery to the
678 intended destination. This preservation shall include identification, handling, packaging, storage and
679 protection. Preservation shall also apply to the constituent parts of a product.

Author's Notes

Clarification—Although it appears to be a relaxation, this clause is simply more concise and less prescriptive yet represents no change of intent.

Remember that handling and/or storage issues are not confined to shipping and receiving areas. This clause could apply anywhere in the facility where material is handled, moved, or stored.

Often stock is assessed for damage and deterioration during the physical inventory. Some items may have a very limited shelf life or require specific environmental conditions, such as temperature, humidity, and so on. Remember to look at *all* storage areas.

Depending on the product, packaging can get very involved to the point of specifying suppliers, stacking heights, means of transportation, and so on.

Common sense is all the standard is really asking for here.

Checklist

A. Do we preserve the conformity of product during internal processing and delivery to the intended destination?
B. Does this preservation include:
    - ❑ Identification?
    - ❑ Handling?
    - ❑ Packaging?
    - ❑ Storage?
    - ❑ Protection?
C. Does this preservation also apply to the constituent parts of a product?

7.6 ~~4.11~~ Control of ~~inspection,~~ monitoring and measuring, ~~and test equipment~~ devices

681 **4.11.1** ~~General~~

682 ~~The supplier shall establish and maintain documented procedures to control, calibrate, and maintain~~
683 ~~inspection, measuring, and test equipment (including test software) used by the supplier to demonstrate~~
684 ~~the conformance of product to the specified requirements~~

685 The organization shall determine the monitoring and measurement to be undertaken and the monitoring
686 and measuring devices needed to provide evidence of conformity of product to determined requirements
687 (see 7.2.1).

688 ~~Inspection, measuring, and test equipment shall be used in a manner which ensures that the measure-~~
689 ~~ment uncertainty is known and is consistent with the required measurement capability.~~

690 The organization shall establish processes to ensure that monitoring and measurement can be carried
691 out and are carried out in a manner that is consistent with the monitoring and measurement requirements.

692 ~~Where the availability of technical data pertaining to the measurement equipment is a specified require-~~
693 ~~ment, such data shall be made available, when required by the customer or customer's representative,~~
694 ~~for verification that the measuring equipment is functionally adequate.~~

695 ~~NOTE 17   For the purposes of this American National Standard, the term "measuring equipment"~~
696 ~~includes measurement devices.~~

697 **4.11.2** ~~Control procedure~~

698 ~~The supplier~~ Where necessary to ensure valid results, measuring equipment shall~~:~~

699 a) ~~determine the measurements to be made and the accuracy required, and select the appropriate~~
700 ~~inspection, measuring, and test equipment that is capable of the necessary accuracy and precision;~~
701 ~~b) identify all inspection, measuring, and test equipment that can affect product quality, and~~ be cali-
702 brated or verified ~~and adjust them~~ at ~~prescribed~~ specified intervals, or prior to use, against ~~certified~~
703 ~~equipment having a known valid relationship~~ measurement standards traceable to internationally or
704 nationally ~~recognized~~ measurement standards; where no such standards exist, the basis used for
705 calibration shall be ~~documented~~ recorded;

706 b) be adjusted or re-adjusted as necessary;

707 c) ~~define the process employed for the calibration of inspection, measuring, and test equipment, includ-~~
708 ~~ing details of equipment type, unique identification, location, frequency of checks, check method, ac-~~
709 ~~ceptance criteria, and the action to be taken when results are unsatisfactory; d) identify inspection,~~
710 ~~measuring, and test equipment with a suitable indicator or approved identification record~~ be identified
711 to ~~show~~ enable the calibration status to be determined;

712 d) ~~i)~~ be safeguarded ~~inspection, measuring, and test facilities, including both test hardware and test~~
713 ~~software,~~ from adjustments ~~which~~ that would invalidate the ~~calibration setting.~~ measurement result;

714 e) ~~h) ensure that the~~ be protected from damage and deterioration during handling, ~~preservation,~~ mainte-
715 nance and storage. ~~of inspection, measuring, and test equipment is such that the accuracy and fit-~~
716 ~~ness for use are maintained;~~

717 ~~g)   ensure that the environmental conditions are suitable for the calibrations, inspections, measurements,~~
718 ~~and tests being carried out;~~

719 In addition, the organization shall ~~f)~~ assess and ~~document~~ record the validity of the previous ~~inspection~~
720 ~~and test~~ measuring results when the ~~inspection, measuring, and test~~ equipment is found not to ~~be out of~~
721 ~~calibration;~~ conform to requirements. The organization shall take appropriate action on the equipment and
722 any product affected. ~~e) maintain calibration records for inspection, measuring, and test equipment~~
723 Records of the results of calibration and verification shall be maintained (see ~~4.16~~ 4.2.4).

724 ~~Where test software or comparative references such as test hardware are used as suitable forms of~~
725 ~~inspection,~~ When used in the monitoring and measurement of specified requirements, ~~they shall be~~

726 ~~checked to prove that they are capable of verifying the acceptability of product,~~ the ability of computer
727 software to satisfy the intended application shall be confirmed. This shall be undertaken prior to ~~release~~
728 ~~for use during production, installation, or servicing,~~ initial use and shall ~~be rechecked~~ reconfirmed at
729 ~~prescribed intervals~~ as necessary. ~~The supplier shall establish the extent and frequency of such checks~~
730 ~~and shall maintain records as evidence of control (see 4.16).~~[1]

731 NOTE ~~18   The metrological confirmation system for measuring equipment given in~~ See ISO 10012–1
732 and ISO 10012–2 ~~may be used~~ for guidance.

Author's Notes

Only measuring and test equipment used to demonstrate conformity of product and conformity of the quality management system, line 738, is required to be under the control of monitoring and measuring devices. In other words, not all equipment has to be calibrated in order to satisfy the standard.

Change—This subclause now specifically requires a process for control, calibration, and maintenance of monitoring and measuring devices. Software used for inspection purposes is also required to be periodically rechecked for capability of verifying product acceptability.

Clarification—Although less prescriptive, the intent remains unchanged from the 1994 version to the 2000 version. Refer to ISO 10012–1 and ISO 10012–2 for further information and guidance. The extent of control may be influenced by such factors as measurement precision, risks involved, industry norms, customer expectations, and so on. Concepts commonly associated with the control of monitoring and measuring devices should be carefully considered. Examples of such concepts are Gage Repeatability & Reproducability, Field of Accuracy Ratios, and Dedicated Calibration Standards.

Checklist

A. Do we determine the monitoring and measurement to be undertaken and the monitoring and measuring devices needed to provide evidence of conformity of product to determined requirements? (see 7.2.1)
B. Do we establish processes to ensure that monitoring and measurement can be carried out?
C. Are monitoring and measurement carried out in a manner that is consistent with the monitoring and measurement requirements?
D. Where necessary to ensure valid results, is measuring equipment:
    - Calibrated or verified at specified intervals, or prior to use, against measurement standards traceable to international or national standards? Where no such standards exist, is the basis used for calibration or verification recorded?
    - Adjusted or re-adjusted as necessary?
    - Identified to enable calibration status to be determined?
    - Safeguarded from adjustments that would invalidate the measurement result?
    - Protected from damage and deterioration during handling, maintenance, and storage?
E. Do we assess and record the validity of the previous measuring results when the equipment is found not to conform to requirements?
F. Do we take appropriate action on the equipment and any product affected?
G. Do we maintain records of the results of calibration and verification? (see 4.2.4)
H. When used in the monitoring and measurement of specified requirements, have we confirmed the ability of computer software to satisfy the intended application?
I. Is this done prior to initial use and reconfirmed as necessary?

---

1. Lines 725–731 were previously 4.11.1, paragraph 2 (1994).

733 **8 ~~4.20~~** ~~Statistical techniques~~ **Measurement, analysis and improvement**

734 **8.1 ~~4.20.1~~** ~~Identification of need~~ **General**

735 The organization shall plan and implement the monitoring, measurement, analysis and improvement
736 processes needed

737 a) to demonstrate conformity of the product,

738 b) to ensure conformity of the quality management system, and

739 c) to continually improve the effectiveness of the quality management system.

740 ~~The supplier~~ This shall include the determination of applicable methods, including ~~identify the need for~~
741 statistical techniques, and the extent of their use ~~required for establishing, controlling, and verifying~~
742 ~~process capability and product characteristics.~~

743 **~~4.20.2~~** ~~Procedures~~

744 ~~The supplier shall establish and maintain documented procedures to implement and control the applica-~~
745 ~~tion of the statistical techniques identified in 4.20.1.~~

Author's Notes

Change—This new clause represents a change in scope and an expansion of intent. Scope now includes all measuring and monitoring going beyond conformity of product to include item b, ensuring "conformity of the quality management system." The intent is further expanded in item c to include continually improving the effectiveness of the quality management system.

Lines 744 and 745, documented procedures are no longer required for statistical techniques, however, objective evidence must exist on how these techniques and the extent of their use are determined.

If certain statistical techniques have become an industry norm, then you should be aware of this. Otherwise, you decide where statistical techniques are appropriate. In identifying need you may wish to consider product, service, process design, process control, problem analysis, determining risk, root cause analysis, product and process limits, forecasting, and verifying quality characteristics. *to measure, analyse + improve*

Examples of statistical techniques that might be covered either in a training manual, a procedure, or work instruction are:
- ❏ Graphical techniques, such as histograms, sequence charts, scatter plots, Pareto diagrams, cause-and-effect diagrams, and so on
- ❏ Statistical control charts
- ❏ Design of experiments
- ❏ Regression analysis
- ❏ Variance analysis
- ❏ Gage R & R

Checklist

A. Do we plan and implement the monitoring, measurement, analysis, and improvement processes needed to:
- ❏ Demonstrate conformity of the product?
- ❏ Ensure conformity of the quality management system?
- ❏ Continually improve the effectiveness of the quality management system?

B. Does this include the determination of applicable methods, including statistical techniques? And the extent of their use?

746 8.2 Monitoring and measurement

747 8.2.1 Customer satisfaction

748 As one of the measurements of the performance of the quality management system, the organization
749 shall monitor information relating to customer perception as to whether the organization has met customer
750 requirements. The methods for obtaining and using this information shall be determined.

Author's Notes

Change—This new requirement goes beyond waiting for a customer to complain to now being proactive in determining customer satisfaction measurements. In order to determine customer satisfaction, organizations may monitor customer perception using a number of methods, such as customer surveys, trip reports of customer visits, benchmarking, and, for companies wishing to be very proactive, the use of quality function deployment (QFD). Monitoring the number of complaints, concessions, returned goods, and customer-generated corrective actions will continue to be used to measure and monitor customer satisfaction.

Checklist

A. As one of the measurements of the performance of the quality management system, do we monitor information relating to customer perception as to whether we have met customer requirements?
B. Have we determined the methods for obtaining and using this information?

751 **8.2.2** ~~4.17~~   **Internal ~~quality~~ audits**

752 The ~~supplier~~ organization shall ~~establish and maintain documented procedures for planning and imple-~~
753 ~~menting~~ conduct internal ~~quality~~ audits at planned intervals to ~~verify~~ determine whether the quality ~~activi-~~
754 ~~ties and related results~~ management system

755 a)   ~~comply with~~ conforms to the planned arrangements (see 7.1), to the requirements of this International
756   Standard and to the quality management system requirements established by the organization, and

757 b)   ~~to determine the effectiveness of the quality system~~ is effectively implemented and maintained.

758 ~~Internal quality~~ An audits program shall be ~~scheduled on the basis of~~ planned, taking into consideration
759 the status and importance of the ~~activity to be audited and shall be carried out by personnel independent~~
760 ~~of those having direct responsibility for the~~ processes and areas to be audited, as well as the results of
761 previous audits. The audit criteria, scope, frequency and methods shall be defined. Selection of auditors
762 and conduct of audits shall ensure objectivity and impartiality of the audit process. ~~activity being audited.~~
763 Auditors shall not audit their own work.

764 The responsibilities and requirements for planning and conducting audits, and for reporting results and
765 maintaining records (see 4.2.4) shall be defined in a documented procedure.

766 ~~The results of the audits shall be recorded (see 4.16) and brought to the attention of the personnel having~~
767 ~~responsibility in the area audited.~~ The management ~~personnel~~ responsible for the area being audited shall
768 ensure that ~~take timely corrective~~ actions are taken without undue delay to eliminate detected nonconfor-
769 mities and their causes ~~on deficiencies found during the audit.~~ Follow-up ~~audit~~ activities shall ~~verify and~~
770 ~~record~~ include the verification ~~implementation and effectiveness~~ of the ~~corrective~~ actions taken ~~(see 4.16).~~
771 and the reporting of verification results (see 8.5.2).

772 NOTES

773 ~~20 The results of internal quality audits form an integral part of the input to management review activities~~
774 ~~(see 4.1.3).~~

775 ~~21 Guidance on quality-system audits is given in~~ See ANSI/ASQC ISO Q10011–1~~–1994~~, ANSI/ASQC
776 Q ISO 10011–2~~–1994,~~ and ANSI/ASQC ISO Q10011–3~~–1994~~ for guidance.

Author's Notes

Clarification—Some companies are concerned about the frequency of internal audits. This will often vary with the maturity of your quality management system. A quality management system should have at least one complete cycle of internal audits prior to a registrar's initial registration audit. A quality management system just starting up may have multiple audit cycles during a year. Many companies rely on one cycle per year. The longest interval would be one complete internal audit cycle in two years. If you are still not sure, consult your registrar.

Clarification—The requirements for auditor independence, lines 759 and 760, are modified in line 763 to simply say "auditors shall not audit their own work."

Clarification—One additional requirement is to establish "follow-up activities" to record the implementation and effectiveness of the corrective action taken. Note the elimination of the word "audit," line 769, from the phrase "follow-up audit activities." This eliminates confusion and no longer implies that a follow-up audit will be performed. Although a follow-up audit may be a value-added activity for assessing effectiveness of complex corrective actions, a follow-up audit is not the only means of determining implementation and effectiveness of actions taken.

NOTE 20, line 773, from the 1994 version has been "upgraded" to a shall statement in 5.6.2a, line 329. Results of internal audits form an integral part of management review activities.

Change—Lines 758–761, requiring the audit of processes are new and may have a significant effect on some organizations. The complexity, number, and identification of processes will determine the extent of the impact. For many companies, the process approach will have no impact whatsoever. These companies have audited processes routinely for some time by digging in and trying to understand processes encountered during the internal audits.

Checklist

A. Do we conduct internal audits at planned intervals to determine whether the quality management system:
- ❏ Conforms to the planned arrangements? (see 7.1)
- ❏ Conforms to the requirements of ISO 9001:2000?
- ❏ Conforms to the quality management system requirements established by our organization?
- ❏ Has been effectively implemented and maintained?

B. Have we planned the audit program, taking into consideration the:
- ❏ Status and importance of the processes and areas to be audited?
- ❏ Results of previous audits?

C. Have we defined the audit:
- ❏ Criteria?
- ❏ Scope?
- ❏ Frequency?
- ❏ Methods?

D. How does the selection of auditors and conduct of audits ensure objectivity and impartiality of the audit process?

E. Do auditors audit their own work?

F. Have we documented a procedure defining the responsibilities and requirements for:
- ❏ Planning and conducting audits?
- ❏ Reporting results?
- ❏ Maintaining records? (see 4.2.4)

G. Does management responsible for the area being audited take actions without undue delay to eliminate detected nonconformities and their causes?

H. Do follow-up activities include the:
- ❏ Verification of the actions taken?
- ❏ Reporting of verification results? (see 8.5.2)

8.2.3　Monitoring and measurement of processes

778 The organization shall apply suitable methods for monitoring and, where applicable, measurement of the
779 quality management system processes. These methods shall demonstrate the ability of the processes
780 to achieve planned results. When planned results are not achieved, correction and corrective action shall
781 be taken, as appropriate, to ensure conformity of the product.

Author's Notes

Change—This clause can be viewed as an expansion of scope to include monitoring all quality management system processes, not just processes for product realization.

Annex B cites 8.2.3 as corresponding to 4.17 Internal quality audits in the 1994 version. This would suggest that monitoring the quality management system includes internal audits.

Further, Annex B cites correspondence to 4.20.1 and 4.20.2 in *ISO 9001:1994,* suggesting that statistical techniques are related to in monitoring and measurement of processes. Statistical techniques are mentioned in lines 740 and 741.

Checklist

A.　Do we apply suitable methods for monitoring and, where applicable, measurement of the quality management system processes?
B.　Do our methods demonstrate the ability of the processes to achieve planned results?
C.　When planned results are not achieved, are correction and corrective action taken, as appropriate, to ensure conformity of the product?

---

782 ## 8.2.4 4.10　Inspection and testing Monitoring and measurement of product

783 ### 4.10.1　General

784 The supplier organization shall establish and maintain documented procedures for inspection and testing
785 activities in order to verify that the specified monitor and measure the characteristics of the product to
786 verify that product requirements for the product are have been met. The required inspection and testing,
787 and the records to be established, shall be detailed in the quality plan or documented procedures. This
788 shall be carried out at appropriate stages of the product realization process in accordance with the
789 planned arrangements (see 7.1).

790 ### 4.10.3　In-process inspection and testing

791 The supplier shall:

792 a)　inspect and test the product as required by the quality plan and/or documented procedures;

793 b)　hold product until the required inspection and tests have been completed or necessary reports have
794 　　been received and verified, except when product is released under positive-recall procedures (see
795 　　4.10.2.3). Release under positive-recall procedures shall not preclude the activities outlined in
796 　　4.10.3a.

797 ### 4.10.4　Final inspection and testing

798 The supplier shall carry out all final inspection and testing in accordance with the quality plan and/or
799 documented procedures to complete the evidence of conformance of the finished product to the specified
800 requirements.

801 The quality plan and/or documented procedures for final inspection and testing shall require that all
802 specified inspection and tests, including those specified either on receipt of product or in-process, have
803 been carried out and that the results meet specified requirements.

804 **4.10.5** ~~Inspection and test records~~

805 ~~The supplier shall establish and maintain records which provide evidence that the product has been~~
806 ~~inspected and/or tested. These records shall show clearly whether the product has passed or failed the~~
807 ~~inspections and/or tests according to defined acceptance criteria. Where the product fails to pass any~~
808 ~~inspection and/or test, the procedures for control of nonconforming product shall apply (see 4.13).~~

809 Evidence of conformity with the acceptance criteria shall be maintained. Records shall ~~identify the inspec~~
810 ~~tion~~ indicate the person(s) ~~authority responsible for the~~ authorizing release of product (see ~~4.16~~ 4.2.4).

811 ~~No~~ Product ~~shall be dispatched~~ release and service delivery shall not proceed until ~~all~~ the ~~activities speci~~
812 ~~fied in the quality plan and/or documented procedures~~ planned arrangements (see 7.1) have been satis-
813 factorily completed, ~~and the associated data and documentation are available and authorized~~ unless
814 otherwise approved by a relevant authority and, where applicable, by the customer.[1]

Author's Notes

Clarification—Although much less prescriptive, there is no real change of overall intent.

This clause does not preclude the use of dock-to-stock or ship-to-stock suppliers. Incoming inspection and test may be waived if you have a means of evaluating and qualifying suppliers to ensure requirements are met.

Lines 791–796 previously indicated that you must have traceability of uninspected product (material) in order to permit "positive recall," line 794, of that material should the material later be found to be nonconforming. The 2000 version does not specifically mention "positive recall." We should not conclude that there may not be a place for positive recall provision within the quality management system. You must still indicate the person(s) authorizing release. This could be obvious in the process or designated in job instructions, marked on a traveler, or included in other documentation (records).

Change—Lines 809 and 810 state that "Records shall indicate the person(s) authorizing release of product" (see 4.2.4). Note this does not require the identification of those persons on the product itself.

Checklist

A. Do we monitor and measure the characteristics of the product to verify that product requirements have been met?
B. Is the monitoring and measuring of the product characteristics carried out at appropriate stages of the product realization process in accordance with the planned arrangements? (see 7.1)
C. Do we maintain evidence of conformity with the acceptance criteria?
D. Do our records indicate the person(s) authorizing release of product? (see 4.2.4)
E. Do we ensure that product release and service delivery does not proceed until the planned arrangements (see 7.1) have been satisfactorily completed, unless otherwise approved by a relevant authority, and where applicable, by the customer?

---

1. Lines 812–815 were previously 4.10.4, paragraph 3 (1994).

8.3 ~~4.13~~ Control of nonconforming product

~~4.13.1~~ ~~General~~

The ~~supplier~~ organization shall ~~establish and maintain documented procedures to~~ ensure that product ~~that which~~ does not conform to ~~specified~~ product requirements is ~~prevented from~~ identified and controlled to prevent its unintended use or ~~installation~~ delivery. ~~This~~ The controls and related responsibilities and authorities for dealing with nonconforming product shall ~~provide for identification, documentation, evaluation, segregation (when practical), disposition of nonconforming product, and for notification to the functions concerned~~ be defined in a documented procedure.

~~4.13.2~~ ~~Review and disposition of nonconforming product~~

~~The responsibility for review and authority for the disposition of nonconforming product shall be defined.~~

The organization shall deal with nonconforming product ~~shall be reviewed in accordance with documented procedures. It may~~ be by one or more of the following ways:

a) ~~reworked to meet the specified requirements,~~ by taking action to eliminate the detected nonconformity;

b) ~~accepted with or without repair by concession,~~ by authorizing its use, release or acceptance under concession by a relevant authority and, where applicable, by the customer;

c) ~~regraded for alternative applications, or d) rejected or scrapped~~ by taking action to preclude its original intended use or application.

~~Where required by the contract, the proposed use or repair of product (see 4.13.2b) which does not conform to specified requirements shall be reported for concession to the customer or customer's representative. The description of the nonconformity that has been accepted, and of repairs, shall be recorded to denote the actual condition (see 4.16).~~

Records of the nature of nonconformities and any subsequent actions taken, including concessions obtained, shall be maintained (see 4.2.4).

~~Repaired and/or reworked product shall be reinspected in accordance with the quality plan and/or documented procedures.~~

When nonconforming product is corrected it shall be subject to re-verification to demonstrate conformity to the requirements.

When nonconforming product is detected after delivery or use has started, the organization shall take action appropriate to the effects, or potential effects, of the nonconformity.

Author's Notes

This clause applies to both in-house production and vendor-supplied material. Anything out of specification is considered nonconforming and you must have a means of dealing with it.

You need to have a means of dealing with nonconformities that is acceptable to your customer.

The title of this clause has been slightly modified to be more specific. The change in title reflects that every nonconformity that results in nonconforming product is dealt with in this subclause.

The term "identified" indicates that identification of nonconforming product must be clear throughout all processes. This identification is frequently in the form of tags, labels, move tickets, location, inspection reports, and so on.

Change—The last two lines of clause 8.3 represent a change from the 1994 version. At lines 873 and 874, clause 4.14.2a of the 1994 version required "effective handling of customer complaints and reports of product nonconformities," while the 2000 version, lines 843 and 844, requires the organization to "take action appropriate to the effects, or potential effects, of the nonconformity." Such action might include notifying customers and/or regulatory authorities of nonconformities and, where appropriate, of any product recalls.

Checklist

A. Do we ensure that product which does not conform to product requirements is identified and controlled to prevent its unintended use or delivery?
B. Do we have a documented procedure for controls and related responsibilities and authorities for dealing with nonconforming product?
C. Do we deal with nonconforming product in one or more of the following ways:
   - ❏ By taking action to eliminate the detected nonconformity?
   - ❏ By authorizing its use, release, or acceptance under concession by a relevant authority and, where applicable, by the customer?
   - ❏ By taking action to preclude its original intended use or application?
D. Do we maintain records of the nature of nonconformities and any subsequent actions taken, including concessions obtained? (see 4.2.4)
E. After nonconforming product is corrected, do we re-verify it to demonstrate conformity to requirements?
F. When nonconforming product is detected after delivery or use has started, do we take action appropriate to the effects or potential effects of the nonconformity?

845 **8.4**   **Analysis of data**

846 The organization shall determine, collect and analyze appropriate data to demonstrate the suitability and
847 effectiveness of the quality management system and to evaluate where continual improvement of the
848 effectiveness of the quality management system can be made. This shall include data generated as a
849 result of monitoring and measurement and from other relevant sources.

850 The analysis of data shall provide information relating to

851 a)   customer satisfaction (see 8.2.1),

852 b)   conformity to product requirements (see 7.2.1),

853 c)   characteristics and trends of processes and products including opportunities for preventive action,
854   and

855 d)   suppliers.

Author's Notes

Change—Analysis of data is a new requirement in the 2000 version that data and trends must be analyzed. This new clause is simply stating that which was implied at 4.1.3b and at 4.14.3a in the 1994 version. The term "analysis" is a change and has a different meaning than terms in the 1994 version such as "monitoring" and "collecting data."

Checklist

A.   Do we determine, collect, and analyze appropriate data to demonstrate the suitability and effectiveness of the quality management system? And to evaluate where continual improvement of the quality management system can be made?

B.   Does this include data generated as a result of monitoring and measurement and from other relevant sources?

C.   Do we analyze this data to provide information relating to:
- ❑   Customer satisfaction? (see 8.2.1)
- ❑   Conformance to product requirements? (see 7.2.1)
- ❑   Characteristics and trends of processes and products, including opportunities for preventive action?
- ❑   Suppliers?

856 **8.5**   **Improvement**

857 **8.5.1**   **Continual improvement**

858 The organization shall continually improve the effectiveness of the quality management system through
859 the use of the quality policy, quality objectives, audit results, analysis of data, corrective and preventive
860 actions and management review.

Author's Notes

Assess objective evidence of continual improvement by searching for improving trends in key measurables by reviewing their history over time. Refer to Figure 1, line 69, to view an illustration of how a process-based quality management system that drives the continual improvement process is built into the structure of ISO 9001:2000.

Management must review continual improvement in management review, lines 324, 335, 338, and 339.

Checklist

A.   Do we continually improve the effectiveness of the quality management system through the use of:
- The quality policy?
- Quality objectives?
- Audit results?
- Analysis of data?
- Corrective and preventive actions?
- Management review?

861 **8.5.2** ~~4.14~~ **Corrective ~~and preventive~~ action**

862 **~~4.14.1~~** **~~General~~**

863 ~~The supplier shall establish and maintain documented procedures for implementing corrective and pre-~~
864 ~~ventive action.~~

865 ~~Any~~ The organization shall take ~~corrective or preventive~~ action ~~taken~~ to eliminate the causes of ~~actual or~~
866 ~~potential~~ nonconformities in order to prevent recurrence. Corrective actions shall be ~~to a degree~~ appropri-
867 ate to the ~~magnitude of problems and commensurate with the risks~~ effects of the nonconformities en-
868 countered.

869 ~~The supplier shall implement and record any changes to the documented procedures resulting from~~
870 ~~corrective and preventive action.~~

871 **~~4.14.2~~** **~~Corrective action~~**

872 ~~The~~ A documented procedures ~~for corrective action~~ shall ~~include~~ be established to define requirements for

873 a)   ~~the effective handling of~~ reviewing nonconformities (including customer complaints), ~~and reports of~~
874   ~~product nonconformities;~~

875 b)   ~~investigation of~~ determining the causes of nonconformities, ~~relating to product, process, and quality~~
876   ~~system, and recording the results of the investigation (see 4.16);~~

877 c)   ~~determination of the corrective action needed to eliminate the cause of nonconformities;~~ evaluating
878   the need for action to ensure that nonconformities do not recur,

879 d)   ~~application of controls to ensure that corrective action is taken and that it is effective.~~ determining and
880   implementing action needed,

881 e)   records of the results of action taken (see 4.2.4), and

882 f)   reviewing corrective action taken.

Author's Notes

Clarification—The revisions to corrective action represent no changes of intent from the 1994 version.

Corrective action and preventive action are placed in separate subclasses. Both were required in the 1994 standard.

Follow-up or review to ensure corrective action effectiveness is essential. Unless it can be shown that a corrective action either failed to close out a customer complaint or failed to rectify a nonconformity, continue to regard the corrective action as effective.

An effective corrective action process is a crucial element in any quality management system. Corrective action is one of the means of driving continual improvement. Although not addressed in the standard, experience shows that thorough root cause analysis and solid problem-solving techniques are a must to actually prevent recurrence.

Checklist

A.   Do we take action to eliminate the cause of nonconformities in order to prevent recurrence?
B.   Is corrective action appropriate to the effects of nonconformities encountered?
C.   Do we have a documented corrective action procedure to define requirements for:
  ❑   Reviewing nonconformities (including customer complaints)?
  ❑   Determining the causes of nonconformities?
  ❑   Evaluating the need for action to ensure that nonconformities do not recur?
  ❑   Determining and implementing action needed?
  ❑   Maintaining records of the results of action taken? (see 4.2.4)
  ❑   Reviewing corrective action taken?

883 **8.5.3** 4.14.3   **Preventive action**

884 The organization shall determine action to eliminate the causes of potential nonconformities in order to
885 prevent their occurrence. Preventive actions shall be appropriate to the effects of the potential problems.

886 ~~The~~ A documented procedures ~~for preventive action~~ shall ~~include~~ be established to define requirements
887 for

888 a) ~~the use of appropriate sources of information such as processes and work operations which affect~~
889   ~~product quality, concessions, audit results, quality records, service reports, and customer complaints~~
890   ~~to detect, analyze, and eliminate potential causes of~~ determining potential nonconformities and their
891   causes,

892 b) ~~determination of the steps needed to deal with any problems requiring preventive~~ evaluating the need
893   for action to prevent occurrence of nonconformities,

894 c) ~~initiation of preventive action and application of controls to ensure that it is effective;~~ determining and
895   implementing action needed,

896 d) ~~ensuring that relevant information on actions taken is submitted for management review (see 4.1.3).~~
897   records of results of action taken (see 4.2.4), and

898 e) reviewing preventive action taken.

Author's Notes

Clarification—You will need a procedure for preventive action. The 2000 version represents no real change of intent from the 1994 version.

The preventive action procedure should reference or closely tie-in with the management review procedure. Clause 5.6.2d, line 332, requires corrective and preventive actions as input to management review. Key indicators and trends are referenced in preventive action, management review, and clause 8.4c of the 2000 version.

Preventive action is taken to eliminate *potential* nonconformities in order to prevent their *occurrence*. Corrective action is taken to eliminate *existing* nonconformities and to prevent their *recurrence*. The approaches for each are often different.

Preventive action must be appropriate "to the effects of potential problems" and commensurate to the risks encountered. While this section has been rewritten and reorganized, the intent is still in agreement with the previous applications of this clause.

Note that the reference to determining "action to eliminate the causes" in line 884, while subtle, implies that multiple causes likely exist. An organization will typically seek out root causes and address them with appropriate countermeasures. A tool, such as failure mode and effects analysis (FMEA), can be useful here.

Checklist

A.   Do we take action to eliminate the causes of potential nonconformities in order to prevent occurrence?
B.   Is preventive action taken appropriate to the effects of the potential problems?
C.   Do we have a documented preventive action procedure which defines requirements for:
    ❑   Determining potential nonconformities and their causes?
    ❑   Evaluating the need for action to prevent occurrence of nonconformities?
    ❑   Determining and implementing action needed?
    ❑   Maintaining records of results of preventive action taken? (see 4.2.4)
    ❑   Reviewing preventive action taken?

Annex A (informative)

Annex B (informative)

Bibliography

[1] ANSI/ASQC Q9000–1–1994, ~~Quality Management and Quality Assurance Standards—Guidelines for Selection and Use.~~

ISO 9000–3:1997, *Quality management and quality assurance standards—Part 3: Guidelines for the application of ISO 9001:1994 to the development, supply, installation and maintenance computer software.*

[2] ANSI/ASQC Q9002–1994, ~~Quality Systems—Model for Quality Assurance in Production, Installation, and Servicing.~~

ISO 9004: –1), *Quality management systems—Guidelines for performance improvements.*

[3] ANSI/ASQC Q9003–1994, ~~Quality Systems—Model for Quality Assurance in Final Inspection and Test.~~

ISO 10005:1995, *Quality management—Guidelines for quality plans.*

[4] ANSI/ASQC Q10011–1–1994, ~~Guidelines for Auditing Quality Systems—Auditing.~~

ISO 10006:1997, *Quality management—Guidelines to quality in project management.*

[5] ANSI/ASQC Q10011–2–1994, ~~Guidelines for Auditing Quality Systems—Qualification Criteria for Quality Systems Auditors.~~

ISO 10007:1995, *Quality management—Guidelines for configuration management.*

[6] ANSI/ASQC Q10011–3–1994, ~~Guidelines for Auditing Quality Systems—Management of Audit Programs.~~

ISO 10011–1:1990, *Guidelines for auditing quality systems—Part 1: Auditing 2).*

[7] ~~ISO 9000–2:1993, Quality management and quality assurance standards—Part 2: Generic guidelines for the application of ISO 9001, ISO 9002 and ISO 9003.~~

ISO 10011–2:1991, *Guidelines for auditing quality systems—Part 2: Qualification criteria for quality systems auditors 2).*

[8] ~~ISO 9000–3:1991, Quality management and quality assurance standards—Part 3: Guidelines for the application of ISO 9001 to the development, supply and maintenance of software.~~

ISO 10011–3:1991, *Guidelines for auditing quality systems—Part 3: Management of audit programs 2).*

[9] ~~ISO 10012–1:1992, Quality assurance requirements for measuring equipment—Part 1: Metrological confirmation system for measuring equipment.~~

ISO 10012–1:1992, *Quality assurance requirements for measuring equipment—Part 1: Metrological confirmation system for measuring equipment 3).*

[10] ~~ISO 10013: –1), Guidelines for developing quality manuals.~~

ISO 10012–1:1997, *Quality assurance for measuring equipment— Part 2: Guidelines for control of measurement processes 3).*

[11] ISO 10013:1995, *Guidelines for developing quality manuals.*

[12] ISO/TR 10014:1998, *Guidelines for managing the economics of quality.*

[13] ISO 10015, *Quality management—Guidelines for training.*

[14] ISO/TR 10017:1999, *Guidelines on statistical techniques for ISO 9001:1994.*

71

940 [15] ISO 14001:1996, *Environmental management system—Specification with guidance for use.*

941 [16] ISO/TC 176/SC 2/N 376, *Quality management principles and guidelines on their application 4).*

942 [17] Reference websites: http://www.iso.ch

943   http://www.bsi.org.uk/iso–tc176–sc2.

944 _____

945 1)   To be published.

946 2)   To be revised as ISO 19011, Guidelines for auditing management systems.

947 3)   To be revised as ISO 10012, Quality assurance requirements for measuring equipment.

948 4)   Available from website: http://bsi.org.uk/iso–tc–sc2, at no charge.

Key Words
(author originated)

949   **4.16 (19)** 242, 326, 361, 391, 430, 500, 506, 546, 570, 623, 642, 652, 723, 730, 766, 770, 810, 836, 876

950   **4.2.4 (22)** 189, 217, 242, 326, 362, 392, 430, 470, 501, 506, 518, 531, 548, 623, 642, 652, 723, 765, 810, 838, 881, 897

951   **AUDIT (12)** 538, 761, 762, 763, 769, 769, 859, 889, 918, 927, 952, 953

952   **AUTHORIZED (4)** 222, 528, 636, 813

953   **CONSISTENT PAIR (2)** 71, 74

954   **CONTINUAL IMPROVEMENT (7)** 55, 79, 81, 100, 170, 847, 857

955   **CONTINUALLY IMPROVE (6)** 68, 159, 274, 346, 739, 858

956   **CUSTOMER DISSATISFACTION (0)**

957   **CUSTOMER REQUIREMENTS (10)** 43, 59, 63, 77, 266, 312, 339, 348, 432, 749

958   **CUSTOMER SATISFACTION (8)** 42, 58, 99, 104, 267, 348, 747, 851

959   **DEFINE RESPONSIBILITY (1)** 454

960   **DESIGN AND DEVELOPMENT (26)** 452, 453, 455, 457, 458, 459, 460, 466, 468, 475, 480, 481, 482, 484, 485, 492, 493, 496, 499,
961   502, 504, 513, 514, 525, 526, 528

962   **DOCUMENT (14)** 122, 127, 128, 158, 212, 214, 215, 217, 218, 228, 269, 374, 400, 719

963   **DOCUMENTATION (9)** 23, 179, 182, 195, 200, 209, 385, 813, 820

964   **DOCUMENTED (53)** 183, 185, 187, 190, 192, 193, 207, 218, 234, 247, 295, 354, 377, 396, 399, 408, 423, 431, 450, 464, 470, 481,
965   493, 526, 534, 565, 591, 597, 606, 628, 634, 641, 646, 659, 682, 705, 744, 752, 765, 784, 787, 792, 798, 801, 812, 817, 822, 825,
966   839, 863, 869, 872, 886

967   **DOCUMENTED PROCEDURES (36)** 185, 187, 190, 207, 234, 247, 354, 399, 408, 450, 534, 565, 591, 597, 606, 628, 634, 641,
968   646, 659, 682, 744, 752, 784, 787, 792, 798, 801, 812, 817, 825, 870, 862, 860, 872, 886

969   **DOCUMENTS (24)** 187, 200, 212, 216, 219, 220, 222, 223, 224, 227, 229, 230, 233, 234, 236, 238, 239, 382, 437, 491, 512, 550
970   558, 577

971   **EFFECTIVE (12)** 99, 166, 188, 231, 244, 443, 464, 583, 873, 879, 894, 972

972   **EFFECTIVELY (3)** 44, 187, 757

973   **EFFECTIVENESS (19)** 42, 54, 76, 80, 160, 258, 274, 317, 323, 338, 346, 358, 739, 757, 770, 847, 847, 858, 973

974   **ESTABLISH (28)** 63, 90, 158, 203, 234, 247, 354, 381, 408, 450, 534, 546, 572, 606, 617, 628, 640, 646, 659, 682, 690, 729, 744,
975   752, 784, 805, 817, 863

976   **ESTABLISHED (17)** 108, 193, 208, 219, 243, 248, 251, 262, 283, 308, 316, 443, 547, 756, 787, 872, 886

977   **ESTABLISHES (0)**

978   **ESTABLISHING (3)** 261, 276, 741

979   **IDENTIFY RESPONSIBILITY (0)**

980   **IMPROVE (6)** 68, 159, 274, 346, 739, 858

981   **IMPROVE ITS EFFECTIVENESS (2)** 159, 346

982   **IMPROVE THE EFFECTIVENESS (3)** 274, 739, 858

983   **IMPROVEMENT (15)** 55, 79, 81, 100, 170, 311, 324, 335, 338, 339, 733, 735, 847, 856, 857

984   **INTERNATIONAL (28)** 22, 24, 31, 34, 41, 60, 73, 84, 86, 88, 91, 94, 102, 113, 115, 117, 123, 126, 130, 134, 140, 150, 160, 172,
985   186, 189, 192, 755

986 **MAINTAIN (28)** 129, 158, 203, 234, 247, 346, 354, 361, 364, 408, 450, 534, 546, 606, 628, 641, 646, 659, 682, 682, 722, 730, 744,
987 752, 784, 805, 817, 863

988 **MAINTAINED (24)** 193, 243, 277, 289, 309, 326, 361, 429, 470, 500, 506, 518, 527, 530, 548, 622, 634, 644, 652, 716, 723, 757,
989 809, 838

990 **MAINTAINING (1)** 765

991 **MAINTAINS (0)**

992 **MAINTENANCE (7)** 249, 489, 604, 647, 714, 905, 926

993 **MANAGEMENT SYSTEM (62)** 18, 19, 22, 24, 42, 51, 56, 69, 71, 75, 77, 78, 83, 86, 89, 89, 90, 90, 95, 131, 156, 158, 162, 176, 177,
994 182, 195, 205, 208, 210, 216, 244, 258, 275, 285, 287, 289, 289, 308, 310, 314, 317, 321, 325, 334, 338, 346, 376, 400, 557, 738,
995 739, 748, 754, 756, 779, 847, 848, 858, 909, 940, 946

996 **MAY (14)** 36, 143, 190, 254, 313, 382, 398, 403, 507, 522, 524, 612, 732, 826

997 **MEASURED (0)**

998 **MEASUREMENT (25)** 55, 178, 387, 602, 611, 638, 685, 688, 689, 690, 691, 692, 696, 703, 704, 713, 725, 733, 735, 746, 777, 778,
999 782, 849, 935

1000 **MEASUREMENT PROCESS (1)** 935

1001 **MEASURES (1)** 505

1002 **NOTE (23)** 29, 61, 102, 111, 177, 190, 192, 194, 200, 211, 254, 313, 398, 400, 403, 439, 442, 507, 625, 643, 655, 695, 731

1003 **NOTES (3)** 142, 519, 772

1004 **ORGANIZATION (95)** 18, 19, 20, 21, 32, 32, 44, 47, 59, 64, 79, 88, 90, 96, 116, 118, 138, 139, 158, 161, 163, 172, 174, 175, 188,
1005 195, 197, 203, 259, 273, 277, 283, 291, 295, 312, 316, 321, 343, 354, 364, 370, 374, 378, 396, 403, 411, 416, 418, 419, 426, 433,
1006 436, 436, 442, 443, 453, 457, 462, 534, 542, 544, 558, 572, 575, 576, 588, 609, 617, 628, 638, 640, 646, 648, 649, 649, 677, 685,
1007 690, 719, 721, 735, 748, 749, 752, 756, 778, 784, 817, 825, 843, 846, 858, 865, 884, 999

1008 **POLICY FOR QUALITY (1)** 269

1009 **PREVENTIVE MAINTENANCE (0)**

1010 **PROCEDURE (6)** 192, 193, 218, 697, 765, 822

1011 **PROCEDURES (46)** 181, 185, 187, 190, 195, 207, 234, 247, 354, 385, 399, 408, 450, 534, 554, 565, 591, 592, 597, 606, 621, 628,
1012 634, 641, 646, 659, 682, 743, 744, 752, 784, 787, 792, 794, 795, 799, 801, 808, 812, 817, 826, 840, 863, 869, 872, 886

1013 **PROCESS (35)** 40, 41, 46, 46, 48, 49, 54, 56, 56, 68, 69, 174, 297, 299, 331, 367, 384, 463, 533, 553, 555, 587, 599, 604, 614, 616,
1014 625, 707, 741, 762, 788, 790, 802, 875, 1005

1015 **PROCESSES (65)** 20, 47, 48, 50, 50, 53, 55, 60, 61, 63, 65, 66, 99, 141, 162, 164, 165, 168, 169, 170, 172, 175, 175, 177, 177,
1016 188, 198, 209, 308, 316, 338, 374, 376, 381, 392, 400, 401, 404, 405, 555, 589, 589, 601, 608, 609, 610, 611, 613, 615, 617, 619,
1017 622, 625, 626, 669, 690, 735, 760, 777, 779, 779, 853, 888, 935, 1007

1018 **QUALITY (198)** 2, 3, 3, 4, 7, 7, 11, 11, 15, 15, 18, 19, 22, 24, 27, 28, 33, 36, 38, 42, 51, 56, 69, 71, 75, 76, 78, 89, 90, 0, 0, 94, 95,
1019 131, 131, 156, 158, 162, 176, 177, 179, 181, 182, 183, 183, 184, 186, 187, 195, 202, 203, 205, 207, 207, 208, 210, 211, 216, 231,
1020 242, 243, 244, 245, 249, 250, 251, 251, 258, 261, 262, 268, 269, 270, 270, 270, 272, 275, 276, 281, 282, 283, 284, 285, 287, 288,
1021 289, 289, 294, 297, 299, 308, 310, 311, 314, 317, 321, 324, 325, 325, 334, 338, 345, 346, 351, 356, 360, 375, 375, 376, 380, 380,
1022 383, 385, 391, 395, 395, 398, 399, 400, 402, 537, 538, 538, 544, 545, 546, 557, 564, 583, 589, 592, 597, 634, 675, 701, 738, 739,
1023 748, 751, 753, 753, 756, 757, 758, 773, 775, 779, 787, 792, 798, 801, 812, 839, 847, 848, 858, 859, 859, 875, 889, 889, 902, 902,
1024 904, 904, 907, 907, 909, 910, 910, 912, 912, 913, 914, 914, 915, 916, 917, 918, 920, 921, 921, 923, 923, 925, 925, 927, 929, 931,
1025 933, 934, 936, 937, 938, 941, 947, 1020, 1021

1026 **QUALITY MANAGEMENT SYSTEM (55)** 18, 19, 22, 24, 42, 51, 56, 69, 71, 75, 76, 78, 89, 90, 95, 131, 156, 158, 162, 176, 177,
1027 182, 195, 205, 208, 210, 216, 244, 258, 275, 285, 287, 289, 289, 308, 310, 314, 317, 321, 324, 334, 338, 346, 376, 400, 557, 738,
1028 739, 748, 756, 779, 847, 848, 858, 909

1029 **QUALITY MANUAL (7)** 184, 202, 203, 207, 211, 933, 936

1030 **QUALITY OBJECTIVE (11)** 183, 262, 276, 281, 282, 283, 288, 325, 360, 380, 859

1031 **QUALITY OBJECTIVES (11)** 183, 262, 276, 281, 282, 283, 288, 325, 360, 380, 859

1032 **QUALITY PLAN (16)** 375, 380, 398, 402, 564, 597, 634, 787, 792, 798, 801, 812, 839, 912, 1020, 1021

1033 **QUALITY POLICY (9)** 183, 186, 261, 268, 270, 272, 284, 325, 859

74

1034 **QUALITY SYSTEM (28)** 7, 11, 15, 27, 28, 0, 179, 187, 207, 231, 297, 299, 311, 395, 399, 544, 757, 875, 907, 910, 913, 915, 916,
1035 918, 920, 923, 923, 927

1036 **RECORD (7)** 299, 641, 710, 719, 770, 869, 1023

1037 **RECORDED (10)** 251, 506, 567, 570, 642, 651, 705, 766, 835, 1024

1038 **RECORDS (42)** 189, 216, 242, 243, 245, 249, 250, 251, 252, 254, 326, 361, 391, 391, 428, 429, 470, 500, 505, 517, 527, 530, 538,
1039 546, 547, 622, 623, 652, 722, 722, 730, 765, 787, 804, 805, 806, 809, 837, 881, 889, 897, 1025

1040 **REQUIRE (2)** 613, 801

1041 **REQUIRED (18)** 102, 107, 186, 189, 216, 352, 383, 389, 499, 636, 689, 693, 699, 741, 786, 792, 793, 833

1042 **REQUIREMENT (8)** 29, 115, 387, 421, 431, 606, 640, 692

1043 **REQUIREMENTS (135)** 2, 4, 9, 13, 16, 24, 26, 26, 32, 36, 43, 52, 57, 59, 60, 64, 66, 75, 77, 81, 86, 89, 91, 94, 98, 101, 104, 107,
1044 113, 118, 119, 154, 156, 157, 159, 160, 172, 174, 179, 184, 185, 203, 217, 235, 244, 260, 266, 274, 282, 287, 312, 323, 339, 343,
1045 348, 365, 371, 374, 376, 379, 380, 392, 393, 395, 403, 410, 412, 412, 414, 415, 416, 417, 418, 423, 424, 427, 132, 432, 436, 438,
1046 451, 469, 469, 472, 473, 475, 477, 478, 483, 485, 490, 496, 505, 516, 535, 544, 545, 553, 554, 556, 557, 559, 564, 564, 571, 573,
1047 582, 607, 614, 616, 623, 638, 670, 684, 686, 691, 721, 725, 750, 755, 756, 764, 786, 799, 803, 818, 827, 834, 842, 852, 872, 886,
1048 929, 931, 947

1049 **REQUIREMENTS SPECIFIED BY THE CUSTOMER (1)** 412

1050 **REQUIRES (1)** 58

1051 **REVIEW (31)** 225, 227, 227, 311, 319, 321, 324, 327, 328, 336, 337, 406, 408, 417, 418, 418, 429, 439, 440, 459, 479, 492, 528,
1052 530, 558, 619, 773, 823, 824, 860, 896

1053 **SEE 4.16 (18)** 326, 361, 391, 429, 500, 506, 546, 570, 622, 642, 652, 723, 730, 766, 770, 810, 836, 876

1054 **SEE 4.2.4 (12)** 189, 362, 392, 470, 518, 530, 548, 623, 765, 838, 881, 897

1055 **SERVICE (11)** 143, 151, 486, 586, 587, 588, 608, 609, 612, 811, 889

1056 **SHALL (216)** 158, 161, 172, 175, 176, 182, 203, 207, 216, 217, 219, 221, 222, 224, 226, 228, 234, 243, 245, 245, 247, 247, 250,
1057 251, 252, 257, 266, 269, 270, 271, 282, 284, 286, 293, 294, 305, 306, 316, 321, 324, 326, 328, 337, 343, 351, 354, 361, 364, 370,
1058 374, 375, 377, 378, 395, 396, 408, 411, 418, 418, 421, 421, 429, 432, 435, 437, 443, 450, 453, 454, 455, 457, 462, 463, 466, 470,
1059 471, 470, 177, 170, 181, 182, 484, 491, 494, 498, 500, 503, 506, 514, 517, 518, 526, 527, 529, 530, 534, 536, 542, 547, 548, 550,
1060 558, 562, 564, 566, 570, 572, 576, 580, 582, 584, 585, 588, 589, 590, 594, 606, 606, 010, 012, 616, 617, 617, 622, 628, 632, 634,
1061 638, 640, 642, 646, 649, 651, 659, 662, 664, 666, 667, 669, 672, 675, 676, 677, 678, 679, 682, 685, 688, 690, 693, 698, 705, 719,
1062 721, 723, 725, 727, 727, 728, 729, 730, 735, 740, 744, 749, 750, 752, 758, 759, 761, 762, 763, 765, 766, 767, 769, 778, 779, 780,
1063 784, 787, 787, 791, 795, 798, 801, 805, 806, 808, 809, 809, 811, 811, 817, 820, 824, 825, 825, 834, 835, 838, 839, 841, 843, 846,
1064 848, 850, 858, 863, 865, 866, 869, 872, 884, 885, 886

1065 **SHOULD (3)** 18, 177, 443

1066 **SOFTWARE (8)** 143, 367, 683, 713, 724, 727, 905, 926

1067 **SUBCONTRACT (1)** 543

1068 **SUBCONTRACTED (3)** 537, 579, 581

1069 **SUBCONTRACTOR (7)** 140, 250, 567, 574, 576, 581, 583

1070 **SUBCONTRACTORS (5)** 536, 539, 541, 543, 546

1071 **SUPPLIER (88)** 5, 6, 9, 13, 16, 95, 109, 138, 139, 140, 152, 154, 158, 182, 186, 203, 234, 247, 269, 271, 271, 305, 305, 310, 314,
1072 321, 323, 343, 354, 374, 376, 377, 378, 395, 396, 399, 408, 421, 426, 432, 435, 436, 450, 453, 476, 534, 536, 536, 542, 558, 559,
1073 562, 574, 575, 576, 576, 580, 581, 582, 584, 588, 606, 628, 640, 646, 653, 659, 662, 664, 669, 672, 673, 675, 682, 683, 698, 729,
1074 740, 744, 752, 784, 791, 798, 805, 817, 863, 869, 1037

1075 **SUPPLIERS (2)** 543, 855

1076 **VALIDATE (2)** 609, 1047

Words That Require Definition
(author originated)

1077 **ADEQUATE (4)** 109, 343, 456, 694

1078 **APPROPRIATE (32)** 37, 228, 230, 273, 316, 352, 361, 379, 389, 398, 459, 466, 486, 493, 503, 527, 551, 601, 622, 628, 665, 667,
1079 672, 699, 721, 781, 788, 844, 846, 866, 885, 888

1080 **AUDIT CRITERIA (1)** 761

1081 **AUDIT SCOPE (0)**

1082 **COMMUNICATE (0)**

1083 **COMMUNICATION (9)** 291, 315, 316, 317, 368, 441, 442, 464, 559

1084 **COMPETENT (1)** 351

1085 **CONFORMITY (15)** 100, 117, 174, 244, 331, 364, 370, 677, 686, 737, 738, 781, 809, 841, 852

1086 **CONSIDERATION (5)** 33, 378, 479, 566, 758

1087 **CONTRACT (15)** 152, 154, 401, 406, 408, 421, 424, 426, 429, 434, 435, 442, 479, 580, 833

1088 **CONTRACTUALLY (2)** 251, 676

1089 **CONTROL (36)** 49, 165, 175, 175, 188, 212, 218, 221, 234, 242, 302, 385, 448, 450, 453, 525, 535, 567, 583, 587, 599, 614, 641,
1090 645, 646, 648, 669, 673, 680, 682, 697, 730, 744, 808, 815, 934

1091 **CORRECTIVE ACTION (10)** 332, 768, 770, 780, 866, 871, 872, 877, 879, 882

1092 **CUSTOMER (63)** 32, 42, 43, 58, 58, 59, 63, 77, 97, 99, 100, 103, 104, 119, 138, 154, 236, 252, 252, 259, 265, 266, 267, 312, 330,
1093 339, 348, 348, 405, 412, 414, 419, 431, 432, 441, 442, 447, 447, 575, 579, 580, 580, 584, 585, 645, 647, 649, 650, 651, 653, 655,
1094 693, 693, 747, 749, 749, 814, 830, 834, 834, 851, 873, 889

1095 **CUSTOMER COMMUNICATION (0)**

1096 **DATA (19)** 200, 212, 214, 215, 222, 224, 234, 250, 549, 550, 551, 592, 609, 613, 845, 846, 848, 850, 850

1097 **DEFINE (10)** 190, 220, 248, 269, 374, 454, 535, 707, 872, 886

1098 **DEFINED (15)** 294, 306, 322, 423, 426, 463, 515, 521, 619, 634, 761, 765, 807, 822, 824

1099 **DEFINED INTERVALS (0)**

1100 **EFFECTIVE (11)** 99, 166, 188, 231, 244, 443, 464, 583, 873, 879, 894

1101 **EFFECTIVENESS (18)** 42, 54, 76, 80, 160, 258, 274, 317, 323, 338, 346, 358, 739, 757, 770, 847, 847, 858

1102 **EFFICIENCY (1)** 79

1103 **EFFICIENT (0)**

1104 **ENSURE CONTROL (1)** 175

1105 **EXECUTIVE (3)** 269, 305, 321

1106 **EXECUTIVE MANAGEMENT (0)**

1107 **EXECUTIVE RESPONSIBILITY (3)** 269, 305, 321

1108 **IDENTIFY THE NEED FOR (1)** 740

1109 **IMPLEMENTATION (9)** 19, 257, 301, 455, 517, 528, 601, 603, 770

1110 **INDEPENDENCE (0)**

1111 **INDEPENDENT (2)** 28, 759

1112 **INTEGRATE (1)** 88

1113 **INTERACTION (3)** 50, 164, 209

1114 **INTERVALS (5)** 322, ~~667~~, 702, ~~729~~, 753

1115 **MANAGEMENT (112)** 18, 19, 22, 24, 33, 42, 48, 51, 56, 69, 71, 75, 77, 78, 80, 83, 86, 87, 87, 87, 88, 89, 89, 90, 90, 95, 131, 156,
1116 158, 162, 176, 177, 178, 182, 195, 205, 208, 210, 216, 244, 255, 256, 257, 258, 263, 266, 269, 275, 282, 285, 286, 287, 289, 289,
1117 293, 304, 305, 306, 308, 310, 310, ~~311~~, 313, 314, 316, 317, 319, 321, 321, 325, 326, 328, 333, 334, 337, 338, 341, 344, 346, 376,
1118 400, 557, 643, 738, 739, 748, 754, 756, 767, ~~773~~, 779, 847, 848, 858, 860, 896, ~~902~~, 904, 909, 912, 914, 914, 917, 917, ~~918~~, ~~921~~,
1119 925, 927, 938, 940, 941, 946

1120 **MANAGEMENT WITH EXECUTIVE RESPONSIBILITY (3)** 269, 305, 321

1121 **NEED (11)** ~~36~~, 53, ~~108~~, ~~295~~, 311, 324, 381, ~~734~~, ~~740~~, 878, 892

1122 **NEEDED (22)** 162, 165, 177, 187, ~~199~~, 220, 248, 282, 308, 344, 364, 370, 375, ~~383~~, ~~388~~, 391, 686, 736, ~~877~~, 880, ~~892~~, 895

1123 **NEEDS (8)** 20, ~~95~~, 97, ~~271~~, 340, ~~355~~, 357, ~~515~~

1124 **OBJECTIVE EVIDENCE (0)**

1125 **OBJECTIVES (16)** 20, 63, 66, 78, 183, 262, ~~270~~, 276, 281, 282, 283, 288, 325, 360, 380, 859

1126 **ORDER (19)** 45, 73, 84, 90, ~~154~~, 287, 421, 424, 426, 431, 432, 439, 446, 451, ~~570~~, 667, 785, 866, 884

1127 **ORGANIZATION (94)** 18, 19, ~~20~~, 21, 32, 32, 44, 47, 59, 64, 79, 88, 90, 96, 115, 118, 138, 139, 158, 161, 163, 172, 174, 175, 188,
1128 195, 197, 203, 259, 273, 277, 283, ~~291~~, 295, 312, 316, 321, 343, 354, 364, 370, 374, 378, 396, 403, 411, 416, 418, 419, 426, 433,
1129 436, 436, 442, 443, 453, 457, 462, 534, 542, 544, 558, 572, 575, 576, 588, 609, 617, 628, 638, 640, 646, 648, 649, 649, 677, 685,
1130 690, 719, 721, 735, 748, 749, 752, 756, 778, 784, 817, 825, 843, 846, 858, 865, 884

1131 **PRACTICABLE (2)** ~~228~~, 516

1132 **PREVENTIVE ACTION (11)** 853, 859, 861, ~~863~~, 865, ~~870~~, 883, 885, ~~886~~, ~~894~~, 898

1133 **PROCESS (34)** 40, 41, 46, 46, 48, 49, 54, 56, 56, 68, 69, 174, ~~297~~, 299, 331, 367, 384, 463, 533, ~~553~~, 555, 587, 599, 604, ~~614~~, ~~616~~,
1134 ~~625~~, ~~707~~, ~~741~~, 762, 788, ~~790~~, 802, ~~875~~

1135 **PROCESSES (64)** 20, 47, 48, 50, 50, 53, 55, 60, 61, 63, 65, 66, 99, ~~141~~, 162, 164, 165, 168, 169, 170, 172, 175, 175, 177, 177,
1136 188, 198, 209, 308, 316, 338, 374, 376, 381, 392, 400, 401, 404, 405, 555, ~~589~~, 589, ~~601~~, 608, 609, ~~610~~, 611, ~~613~~, 615, 617, 619,
1137 ~~622~~, ~~625~~, ~~626~~, 669, 690, 735, 760, 777, 779, 779, 853, 888, 935

1138 **PRODUCT (154)** 26, 66, 67, 95, 97, 102, 102, ~~107~~, ~~109~~, 114, 116, 119, ~~141~~, 143, ~~145~~, ~~147~~, ~~148~~, 150, ~~153~~, ~~159~~, 174, 178, 283, ~~297~~,
1139 ~~299~~, ~~302~~, 331, 339, 351, 356, 365, 371, 372, 373, 375, 375, 378, 380, 383, ~~389~~, 390, 390, 392, 400, 401, 403, 410, 415, 417, 418,
1140 419, 423, 436, 440, 445, ~~451~~, 454, 469, 487, 488, ~~489~~, 515, 517, ~~522~~, ~~523~~, 529, 535, 536, ~~537~~, ~~537~~, ~~537~~, 539, 539, 540, 544, 550,
1141 554, 560, ~~562~~, ~~569~~, 573, ~~575~~, 577, ~~579~~, ~~581~~, 584, 593, ~~600~~, ~~611~~, 612, ~~627~~, 629, 630, ~~632~~, ~~633~~, ~~635~~, ~~635~~, 638, 642, 645, ~~647~~, 650,
1142 ~~650~~, ~~654~~, 656, 660, 662, 665, 667, ~~672~~, ~~672~~, 675, 677, 679, 684, 686, 701, 722, 726, 737, 742, 781, 782, 785, 786, 786, 788, ~~792~~,
1143 ~~793~~, ~~794~~, ~~799~~, 802, 805, 806, 807, 808, 810, 811, 815, 817, 818, 820, 821, 823, 824, 825, 833, 839, 841, 843, 852, ~~874~~, ~~875~~, ~~889~~

1144 **PRODUCTION (20)** 8, ~~10~~, ~~11~~, ~~13~~, 0, ~~110~~, 384, 486, ~~569~~, 586, 587, 588, ~~591~~, 596, 608, 609, 629, 635, ~~728~~, 907

1145 **QUALIFIED (4)** ~~351~~, ~~455~~, ~~613~~, ~~622~~

1146 **QUALIFIES (0)**

1147 **QUALIFY (0)**

1148 **QUALITY PLANNING (1)** 375

1149 **QUALITY PLANS (4)** ~~380~~, ~~398~~, ~~597~~, 912

1150 **READILY (3)** ~~219~~, 233, 245

1151 **RECORD (6)** 299, 641, ~~710~~, 719, ~~770~~, 869

1152 **RECORDED (9)** ~~251~~, ~~506~~, ~~567~~, ~~570~~, 642, ~~651~~, 705, ~~766~~, 835

1153 **RECORDS (41)** 189, 216, 242, 243, 245, 249, ~~250~~, ~~251~~, ~~252~~, ~~254~~, 326, 361, ~~391~~, 391, ~~428~~, 429, 470, 500, 505, 517, 527, 530, ~~538~~,
1154 546, 547, ~~622~~, 623, 652, ~~722~~, 722, ~~730~~, 765, ~~787~~, 804, 805, 806, 809, 837, 881, ~~889~~, 897

1155 **RELEASE (11)** 483, ~~491~~, ~~512~~, ~~559~~, 577, 603, ~~727~~, ~~795~~, 810, 811, 829

1156 **REPORT (1)** 67

1157 **REPORTED (2)** 651, ~~834~~

1158 **REPORTING (4)** 310, ~~607~~, 764, 771

1159 **RESOLVE (0)**

1160 **RESOLVED (2)** 425, 477

1161 **RESOLVES (0)**

1162 **RETRIEVABLE (1)** 246

1163 **SUITABILITY (3)** 279, 322, 846

1164 **SUITABLE (16)** 5, 240, 246, 388, 396, 493, 596, 596, 599, 604, 629, 632, 710, 717, 724, 778

1165 **SUPPLIER (87)** 5, 6, 9, 13, 16, 95, 109, 138, 139, 140, 152, 154, 158, 182, 186, 203, 234, 247, 269, 271, 271, 305, 305, 310, 314,
1166 321, 323, 343, 354, 374, 376, 377, 378, 395, 396, 399, 408, 421, 426, 432, 435, 436, 450, 453, 476, 534, 536, 536, 542, 558, 559,
1167 562, 574, 575, 576, 576, 580, 581, 582, 584, 588, 606, 628, 640, 646, 653, 659, 662, 664, 669, 672, 673, 675, 682, 683, 698, 729,
1168 740, 744, 752, 784, 791, 798, 805, 817, 863, 869

1169 **SYSTEM (81)** 2, 4, 18, 19, 24, 36, 42, 47, 50, 51, 56, 69, 72, 75, 77, 78, 89, 89, 90, 90, 94, 96, 99, 100, 156, 158, 162, 176, 177,
1170 179, 181, 182, 187, 195, 205, 207, 208, 210, 216, 231, 244, 258, 275, 285, 287, 289, 290, 298, 299, 308, 310, 311, 314, 318, 322,
1171 325, 334, 338, 346, 376, 396, 399, 400, 544, 557, 731, 738, 739, 748, 754, 756, 757, 775, 779, 847, 848, 858, 876, 930, 932, 940

1172 **TOP MANAGEMENT (11)** 80, 257, 266, 269, 282, 286, 293, 305, 310, 316, 321

1173 **TRANSFER (0)**

1174 **TRANSFERRED (1)** 435

1175 **VALIDATE (1)** 609

1176 **VALIDATES (0)**

1177 **VALIDATION (11)** 389, 459, 513, 514, 516, 518, 520, 521, 522, 608, 615

1178 **VERIFICATION (27)** 345, 388, 389, 459, 481, 502, 503, 505, 506, 507, 520, 560, 564, 569, 574, 576, 577, 579, 582, 584, 646, 653,
1179 694, 723, 770, 771, 841

1180 **VERIFIES (0)**

1181 **VERIFY (10)** 294, 301, 450, 575, 581, 649, 753, 769, 785, 785

1182 **WORK ENVIRONMENT (2)** 369, 370